Checkered Placemat

HOW TO MAKE ON PAGE 46

Appliquéd Hot Pad

HOW TO MAKE ON PAGE 66

"I go to my grandmother's house in early fall, when fewer people seem to be around and the area takes on a lonely mood. Every day I work with my grandmother, learning about sewing and a lot of other things."

Checkered Coaster

HOW TO MAKE ON PAGE 62

Checkered Pot Holder

HOW TO MAKE ON PAGE 64

Appliquéd Room Shoes

HOW TO MAKE ON PAGE 68

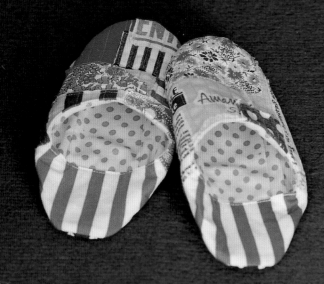

"The first needlework I did was to sew together a pair of room shoes. My grandmother's sewing box contained a large assortment of fabric ends, and in that box, I encountered remnants of dresses and blouses that I had worn as a

Appliquéd Floor Mat

HOW TO MAKE ON PAGE 72

Alphabet Pillow Cover

HOW TO MAKE ON PAGE 76

Checkered Purse

HOW TO MAKE ON PAGE 74

Star Flower Mini Pouch & Log Cabin Mini Pouch

HOW TO MAKE ON PAGES 80 AND 82

"Clothes from my childhood, cloth toys, my favorite stuffed animals, and the coat I had once worn—my grandmother had painstakingly disassembled them and put them away in a box that she treasured. 'All of these are materials for quilts,' she said."

In the Outdoors . . .

" Whenever I'm at my grandmother's house, I head for my
beloved forests, grassy hills, and meadows. I read a book
or collect acorns or wander wooded paths, always with a
quilted item close at hand. "

Appliquéd Mini Bag

HOW TO MAKE ON PAGE 88

Checkered Shoulder Bag

How to make on page 84

Pleated Shoulder Bag

HOW TO MAKE ON PAGE 90

Courthouse Steps Sewing Bag

HOW TO MAKE ON PAGE 94

"A girl should always be neat and well dressed," my grandmother said when she gave me these things, "and in the same
way, you should always take good care of your possessions."

Yo-Yo Glasses Case

HOW TO MAKE ON PAGE 96

Tea Towel Tote Bag

HOW TO MAKE ON PAGE 98

Appliquéd Tote Bag

HOW TO MAKE ON PAGE 100

Hexagon Patchwork Shoulder Bag

HOW TO MAKE ON PAGE 102

"My grandmother taught me to base the color schemes of my patchwork projects on the colors of the flowers and leaves."

Appliquéd Flat Bag

HOW TO MAKE ON·PAGE 110·

Yo-Yo Bag

HOW TO MAKE ON PAGE 106

Hexagon Patchwork Book Cover & Water Bottle Cover

HOW TO MAKE ON PAGES 112 AND 114

Courthouse Steps Quilt

HOW TO MAKE ON PAGE 116

Octagon Patchwork Shoulder Bag

HOW TO MAKE ON PAGE 118

Courthouse Steps Zipper Bag

HOW TO MAKE ON PAGE 122

Getting Started

Patchwork and Quilting Tools

TOOLS FOR PATTERN MAKING

1. Transparent ruler: A long, transparent ruler with parallel lines is helpful when creating large patterns or cutting fabric.
2. Ruler with grid lines: Use a ruler with grid lines and oblique lines when making patterns in various shapes.
3. Short ruler: A short ruler is handy for doing detailed work.
4. Paperweight: A heavy weight will prevent your paper or fabric from slipping when you are making patterns or cutting fabric.
5. Scissors: Use scissors to cut patterns.
6. Pencil: For making patterns and marking fabric, a pencil with B lead (#1 pencil) is most appropriate.
7. Cutting mat: Use this mat when you are cutting patterns or fabric with a rotary cutter.

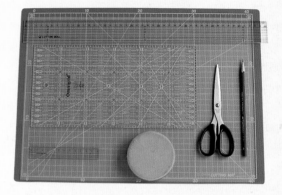

8. Pattern sheet: Make your pattern with this semitransparent paper. Lines and patterns show through, so it's handy for copying pieces or cutting print fabric. Use it by placing the textured side against the fabric.

PINS AND NEEDLES

1. Quilting pins: The ones with the small, round heads are easiest to use for piecing fabric.
2. Appliqué pins: Use shorter pins for appliqué work so they don't get in your way when you sew.
3. Quilting needles: The fine point pierces the fabric easily so you can sew more freely.
4. Appliqué needles: It's easier to stitch appliqué pieces when you use a flexible needle.
5. Basting needles: Use a long, thick, sturdy needle to baste the batting to the fabric when quilting.

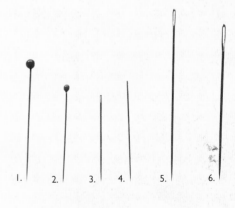

1.   2.   3.   4.   5.   6.

Actual size

6. Embroidery needles: Use this large-eyed needle when you need to work with several strands of embroidery floss at once.

THREAD

a. Quilting thread: Choose a color close to that of the fabric when doing piecework or quilting.

b. Quilting thread: Thread on this type of spool is easier to use.

c. Embroidery floss: This single-strand floss is equivalent to two strands of #25 embroidery floss.

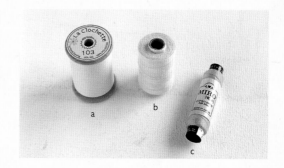

THIMBLES

1, 2, 4. Hard thimbles: Protect your finger when pushing and pulling the needle during quilting work. Thimble (1) is made of metal, (2) of plastic, and (4) is ceramic.

3. Rubber thimble: Wear this type of thimble on the index finger or thumb of your right hand to prevent the thread from slipping when you pull it.

5, 6. Thimble ring: Wear this thimble on the middle finger of your right hand, and use it when pushing and pulling the needle.

OTHER TOOLS

1. Rotary cutter: This tool lets you cut straight lines simply by sliding it over the cloth along a ruler.

2. Spoon: If you hold the fabric down with a spoon while basting, it's easier to work the needle.

3. Stiletto: Use a stiletto to make neat corners or to move fabric along during machine quilting.

4. Sewing scissors: These scissors are used exclusively for cutting fabric.

5. Embroidery scissors: Small scissors with pointed ends are easiest to use when cutting thread.

6. Threader: Use this gadget to thread

needles simply by setting the needle and thread in place and pressing the button.

7. Iron: You'll be ironing small areas, so a small iron is most convenient.

8. Quilting hoop: Setting the fabric in a hoop makes quilting or embroidery work easier.

* In addition, you may find it convenient to have a quilting board (thick paper to which sandpaper has been glued). See steps 1 through 3 in Lesson II.

Patchwork and Quilting Lessons

Let's start by making a placemat with a checkered pattern. We'll go over drawing a pattern, cutting and piecing the fabric, and quilting. At the end of this section, we will review appliqué and machine quilting. Refer back to these lessons when you are making the projects in this book.

CHECKERED PLACEMAT

See the photograph on page 11

Placemat top (48 pieces), Placemat back (1 piece).

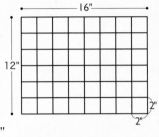

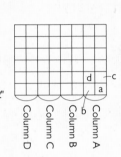

MATERIALS (MAKES 1)

* Fabric for the patchwork (white, assorted patterns): (48) 2¼" × 2¼"
* Fabric for the back: (1) 16¾" × 12¾"
* Fabric for the bias binding (print): (1) 1" × 56⅜"
* Quilt batting: (1) 16¾" × 12¾"

LESSON I

HOW TO MAKE A PATTERN

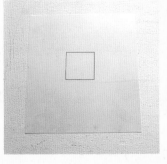

1. Lay a piece of pattern paper down, rough side down, on top of a drawing or an enlarged pattern. Fix it in place with a paperweight, and copy it using a ruler as a guide. Draw the lines along the grain of the fabric.

2. A fully traced pattern. Cut on the lines with scissors or with a rotary cutter using a ruler to guide you. If you have a lot of pattern pieces, label them.

Lesson II
How to Cut the Fabric

1. Lay the fabric on a quilting board (heavy paper to which sandpaper has been glued) wrong side up. Place the pattern down about ⅜" to ¾" from the edge of the fabric. Holding the fabric so that it doesn't slide, use pencil to mark each corner with a dot.

2. The four points marked in black.

3. Remove the pattern, and use a ruler to connect the dots. Make the lines extend a bit beyond the dots.

4. Now you have copied the pattern.

5. Place the fabric on a cutting mat, and cut around the pattern, leaving a seam allowance of ¼". Align the ¼" mark on the ruler with the penciled lines, and cut the fabric with a rotary cutter while pressing down firmly.

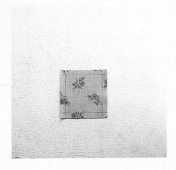

6. The cut piece. If you cut it out with scissors instead of a rotary cutter, use a pencil to draw a seam allowance line ¼" from the edge of the pattern, and cut along that line.

7. This photo shows all 48 pieces cut out with a ¼" seam allowance. Arrange the pieces as you cut them, checking to see that the colors are properly balanced.

Lesson III
How to Sew the Patchwork

This pattern is sewn in sections by columns. In these photographs, we used red thread for greater visibility, but in actual practice, you should use thread that matches the fabric.

a + b
↓

SEWING FABRICS A AND B

b (wrong side)   a (wrong side)

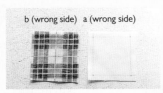

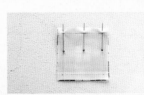

1. First, sew a and b together.
2. Place a and b right sides together, aligning the marks. Pin the pieces together at

the point where you will start sewing, in the middle, and at the point where you will stop sewing.

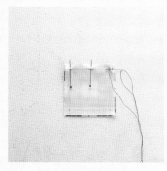

3. Take an appropriate length of thread (about 20"), and make a French knot (see the sidebar on page 63). Insert the needle about ¹⁄₁₆" before the first mark.

4. Backstitch along the marked line (see page 63) to about ¹⁄₁₆" beyond the last mark.

5. If the fabric bunches up, smooth it with your fingers.

6. When you have finished sewing, backstitch once and make a French knot (see the sidebar on page 63) to fix the stitching in place.

7. Fold the seam allowance back toward b, and iron on the right side.

8. View of a and b sewn together, wrong side.

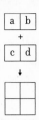

+

↓

SEWING FABRICS A—B AND C—D

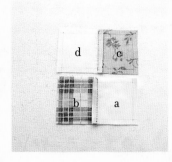

1. Sew fabrics c and d together in the same way as a and b. Fold the seam allowance back toward c, and iron.

2. Place a—b and c—d right sides together, aligning the marks and stitches. Fabrics d and b will be facing each other on the left side; fabrics c and a will be facing each other on the right side. Pin the pieces together.

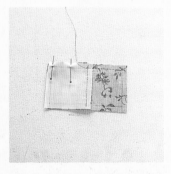

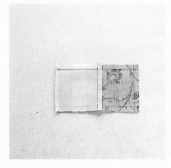

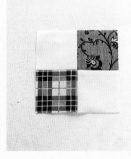

3. Sew as for a—b, stitching the ironed seam allowances in place as you proceed.

4. Backstitch once, and make a French knot ¹/₁₆" beyond the end of the row.

5. Fold the seam allowance back toward a—b, and iron on the right side.

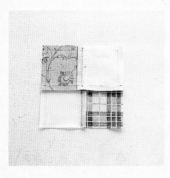

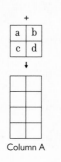

Column A

SEWING COLUMN A

6. Here's what the wrong side will look like.

1. Sew column A together, following the same directions as for Sewing Fabrics a and b and Sewing Fabrics a–b and c–d.

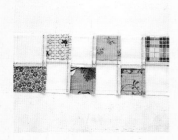

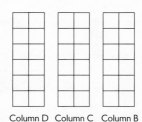

Column D   Column C   Column B

SEWING COLUMNS A, B, C & D

2. Here's what the wrong side will look like. Fold the vertical seam allowances away from each other, and fold the horizontal seam allowances down. Press them in place with an iron.

1. Sew columns B, C, and D in the same way as column A.

2. Here's what the wrong side looks like.

lesson IV
How to Quilt

When quilting, it is essential to work from the center to the outside. Whether you're stitching on horizontal lines or on diagonal lines, your fabric won't bunch up if you work outward from the center.

1. Mark your quilting lines by drawing diagonal lines on the surface of the patchwork fabric with a pencil. Draw parallel lines halfway between these marks.

2. Draw lines running in the opposite direction in the same way.

3. Lay the quilt batting and top fabric on the fabric for the back, and pin all the layers in place. Starting from the center, baste the pieces together horizontally.

4. Continue basting the pieces vertically, working outward from the center. Tip: When you baste, smooth the fabric with a spoon. Lift the tip of the needle with the edge of the spoon to make it easy for the needle to emerge.

5. Place the basted fabric in a hoop. When you sew a small quilt or the edge of a quilt, use an extender, which is simply folded sheeting or a lightweight towel sewn to the edge of the quilt.

6. To start, insert the needle into a stitch near the center of the quilt top, pull it out one stitch ahead of the starting point, and backstitch (see page 63). Continue along the quilting lines with stitches of no more than $1/32$" to $1/12$". Remove basting as you work.

7. Here's what the result will look like.

Lesson V
How to Bind the Quilt

1. To round the corners of the quilt, place a round dish or empty container with a diameter of 2" to 2⅜" on a piece of pattern paper, trace the curve, and cut it out.

2. Place the pattern paper on the corner of the quilt. Draw a curved line, and cut along it.

3. Prepare the bias binding (see the sidebar on page 61). Lay the bias fabric on the quilt about 2¾" to 3" from a corner. Align the cut edges of the quilt fabric and the bias binding, and pin them in place.

4. Start backstitching about 2" in from the edge of the bias binding.

5. Sew all the way around, stopping about 2" short of where you started. Cut the bias binding to the desired measurements.

6. Sew the bias binding together (see the sidebar on page 61), and fold the seam allowances back in one direction. Backstitch the rest of the fabric.

7. Turn the quilt over, and fold the bias binding under to the back. Sew with a blind stitch (see page 63).

8. After you are finished sewing, here's what the wrong side will look like.

9. Here's what the right side will look like.

Lesson VI
How to Machine Appliqué

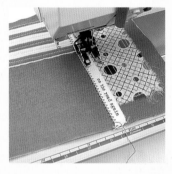

1. Layer the back fabric, quilt batting, and top fabric. Sew the appliqué to the top fabric, machine stitching around the appliqué about ⅛" from the edge of the fabric.

2. Sew different fabrics or tapes in place with the machine; use a zigzag stitch if you wish.

3. If you cut a figure out of a piece of fabric, sew it on with your machine's freestyle function.

4. Continue machine quilting by sewing parallel lines. The distance between the lines depends on the width of the presser foot or your preference.

You can use any scrap of fabric—no matter how small—for appliqué. So save your fabric scraps instead of throwing them away. Instead of cutting the fabric ends neatly with scissors, just make a small cut into the edge and tear the fabric by hand. This gives the scrap a softer edge and appearance.

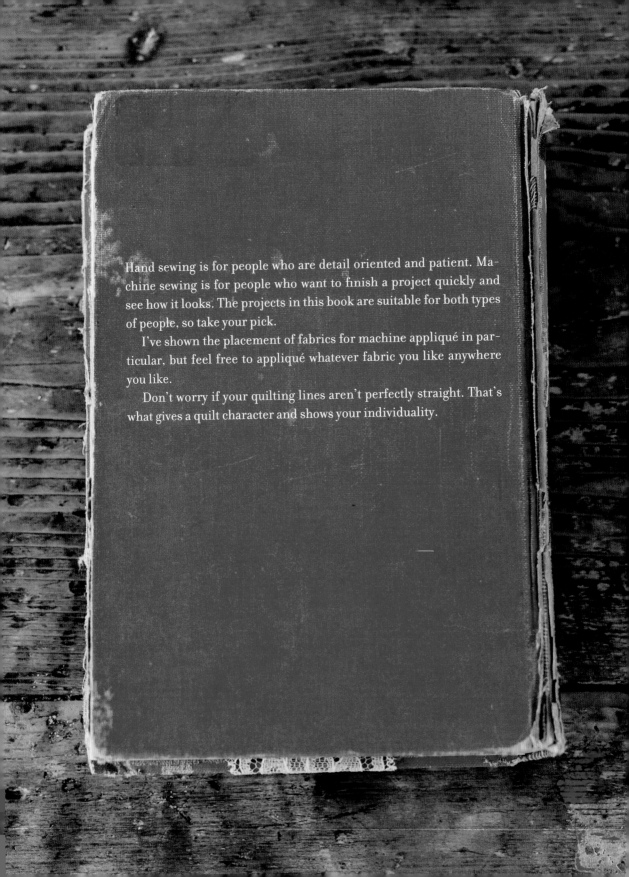

Hand sewing is for people who are detail oriented and patient. Machine sewing is for people who want to finish a project quickly and see how it looks. The projects in this book are suitable for both types of people, so take your pick.

I've shown the placement of fabrics for machine appliqué in particular, but feel free to appliqué whatever fabric you like anywhere you like.

Don't worry if your quilting lines aren't perfectly straight. That's what gives a quilt character and shows your individuality.

How to Make

* Threads are not included in the materials lists. Refer to page 45 when you choose the threads that match your fabric.
* Cut patchwork fabric with a seam allowance of ¼" and other fabric with an allowance of ⅜". The diagrams and patterns represent final measurements without the seam allowance; however, the fabric measurements in the materials lists include the seam allowances.

Checkered Tea Cozy

{SEE PHOTOGRAPH ON PAGE 10}

MATERIALS (MAKES 1)

* Fabric for the patchwork (assorted prints): (60) $2^{1}/_{2}$" × $1^{3}/_{4}$"
* Fabric for top edge (linen): (2) $1^{5}/_{8}$" × $12^{3}/_{4}$"
* Fabric for the bias binding (linen): (1) 1" × $7^{5}/_{8}$", (1) 1" × $24^{3}/_{8}$"
* Quilt batting: (2) $12^{3}/_{4}$" × $8^{1}/_{4}$"
* Fabric for the backing: (2) $12^{3}/_{4}$" × $8^{1}/_{4}$"
* Fabric for lining: (2) $12^{3}/_{4}$" × $8^{1}/_{4}$"

INSTRUCTIONS

1. Following the instructions on pages 46–51, sew the patchwork pieces together to form the patchwork front. You will have six columns of five rectangles.

2. Sew the top edge fabric to the patchwork. Layer the patchwork front, quilt batting, and fabric backing. Mark the quilting lines, and quilt as shown. Repeat steps 1 and 2 for the patchwork back.

3. Place the patchwork front and patchwork back right sides together, and sew the sides. Repeat for the lining front and lining back.

4. Layer the patchwork and lining wrong sides together. Prepare the bias binding (see the sidebar on page 61). Cover the bottom edge with the bias binding following the instructions on page 54–55. Fold in the sides on the top edge.

5. Sew the top edge together, and cover it with bias binding.

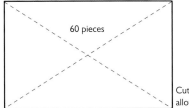

Actual Size Pattern

60 pieces

Cut with a seam allowance of $1/4$"

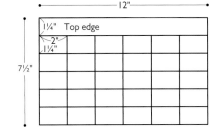

Outer front and back
(1 piece each)

12"

$1^{1}/_{4}$" Top edge

2"

$1^{1}/_{4}$"

$7^{1}/_{2}$"

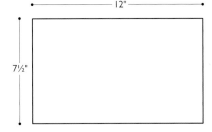

Lining (2 pieces)

12"

$7^{1}/_{2}$"

Cut with a seam allowance of $3/8$"

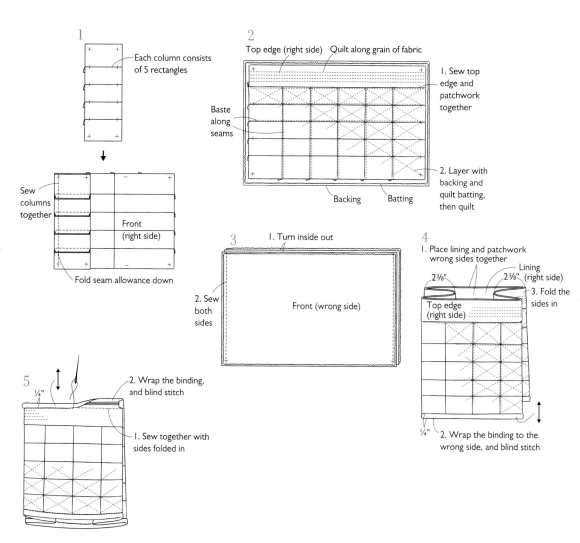

1

Each column consists of 5 rectangles

Sew columns together

Front (right side)

Fold seam allowance down

2

Top edge (right side)   Quilt along grain of fabric

Baste along seams

Backing   Batting

1. Sew top edge and patchwork together

2. Layer with backing and quilt batting, then quilt

3

1. Turn inside out

Front (wrong side)

2. Sew both sides

4

1. Place lining and patchwork wrong sides together

Lining (right side)

2³⁄₈"   2³⁄₈"

3. Fold the sides in

Top edge (right side)

¼"   2. Wrap the binding to the wrong side, and blind stitch

5

¼"

2. Wrap the binding, and blind stitch

1. Sew together with sides folded in

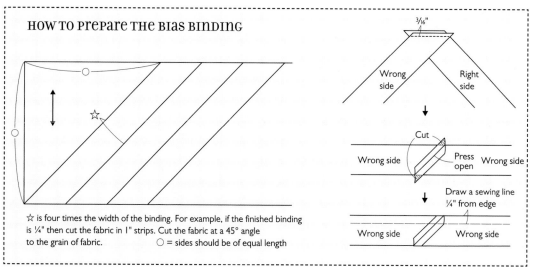

HOW TO PREPARE THE BIAS BINDING

☆ is four times the width of the binding. For example, if the finished binding is ¼" then cut the fabric in 1" strips. Cut the fabric at a 45° angle to the grain of fabric.   ◯ = sides should be of equal length

³⁄₁₆"

Wrong side   Right side

Cut   Press open

Wrong side   Wrong side

Draw a sewing line ¼" from edge

Wrong side   Wrong side

Checkered Coaster

{PHOTOGRAPH ON PAGE 15}

MATERIALS (MAKES 1)

* Fabric for the patchwork (assorted prints): (4) 2¾" × 2¾"
* Fabric for the back: (1) 4¾" × 4¾"
* Quilt batting: (1) 4¾" × 4¾"

INSTRUCTIONS

1. Following the instructions on pages 48–51, sew the patchwork pieces together to form the top of the coaster. You will have one column of two squares.
2. Layer the patchwork top and patchwork back, right sides together, on the quilt batting. Sew around all four sides, leaving a small gap.
3. Turn the piece right side out, and sew the gap closed using a blind stitch (see page 63). Quilt as shown.

Actual Size Pattern
*Pattern can also be used for the Checkered Placemat

Coaster (4 pieces),
Placemat (48 pieces)

Cut with a seam allowance of ¼"

Coaster top (4 pieces),
Coaster back (1 piece)

4"

4"

2"

2"

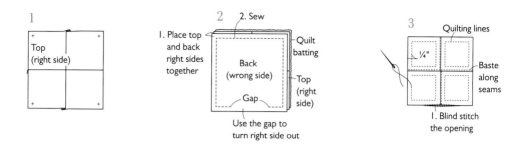

1

Top
(right side)

2 2. Sew

1. Place top
and back
right sides
together

Back
(wrong side)

Quilt
batting

Top
(right
side)

Gap

Use the gap to
turn right side out

3 Quilting lines

¼"

Baste
along
seams

1. Blind stitch
the opening

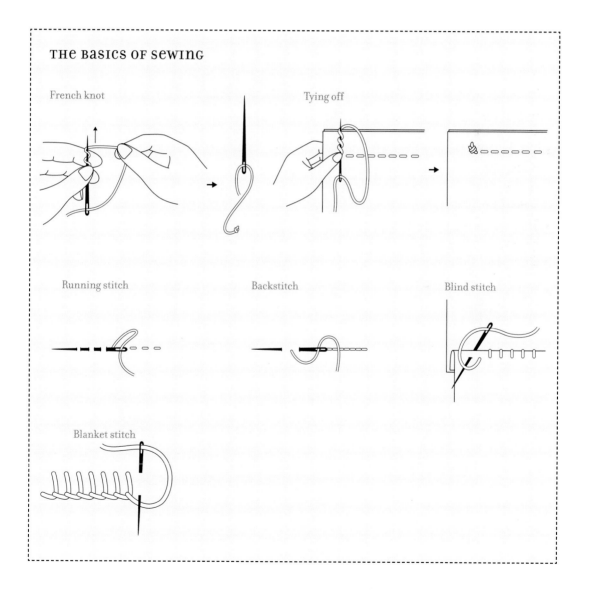

THE BASICS OF SEWING

French knot

Tying off

Running stitch

Backstitch

Blind stitch

Blanket stitch

Checkered Pot Holder

⟩ PHOTOGRAPH ON PAGE 16 ⟨

MATERIALS (MAKES 1)

* Fabric for patchwork (assorted prints): (25) 1¾" × 1¾"
* Fabric for back: (1) 7" × 7"
* Fabric for bias binding: (1) 1½" × 25⅜"
* Quilt batting: (1) 7" × 7"
* Twill tape: (1) ½" × 6"

INSTRUCTIONS

1. Following the detailed instructions for the Checkered Placemat on pages 46–51, sew together five columns of five squares. Layer the back, quilt batting, and top, and quilt as shown. Cut the pot holder to size.

2. Fold the twill tape in half, and baste it to the edge of the pot holder back. Prepare the bias binding (see the sidebar on page 61). Cover the edges with the bias binding following the instructions on pages 54–55. Fold the twill tape up, and sew it in place with a blind stitch.

Actual Size Pattern

25 pieces

Cut with a seam allowance of ¼"

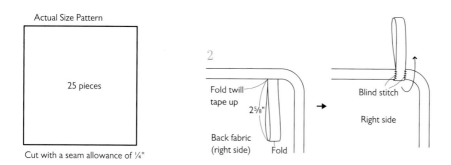

2

Fold twill
tape up

2⅝"

Back fabric
(right side)

Fold

Blind stitch

Right side

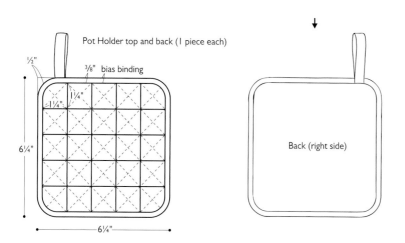

Pot Holder top and back (1 piece each)

½"

⅜" bias binding

1¼"

1¼"

6¼"

6¼"

Back (right side)

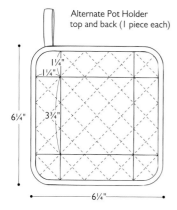

Alternate Pot Holder
top and back (1 piece each)

1¼"

1¼"

6¼"

3¾"

6¼"

Appliquéd Hot Pad
{PHOTOGRAPH ON PAGE 13}

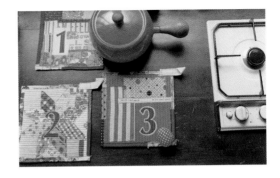

MATERIALS (MAKES 1)

* Fabric for the front and back (linen, cotton, or other): (2) 8" × 8"
* Fabric for appliqué (assorted prints and colors): Scraps and sizes as desired
* Fabric for the bias binding: ¾" to 1" wide in assorted lengths
* Quilt batting: (1) 8" × 8"
* Twill tape: (1) ¾" × 8" to 12"

INSTRUCTIONS

1. Layer the quilt batting and front fabric. Following the instructions on page 56–57, machine appliqué the fabric scraps to the front fabric. Use the designs here, or add the appliqué as you desire. Machine quilt the entire piece.

2. Place the front fabric on the back fabric wrong sides together. Fold the bias binding over the edge, and sew around all four sides.

3. Fold the twill tape in half to create a corner. Place the ends over the pot holder, and sew them in place.

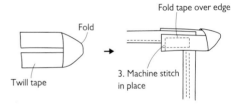

Twill tape — Fold — Fold tape over edge — 3. Machine stitch in place

Enlarge this template by 400%. Use this and the templates on page 67 as guides for sketching and arranging the appliqué pieces.

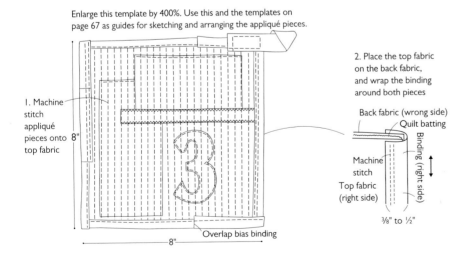

1. Machine stitch appliqué pieces onto top fabric

8"

8"

Overlap bias binding

2. Place the top fabric on the back fabric, and wrap the binding around both pieces

Back fabric (wrong side)
Quilt batting
Machine stitch
Top fabric (right side)
Binding (right side)
⅜" to ½"

66

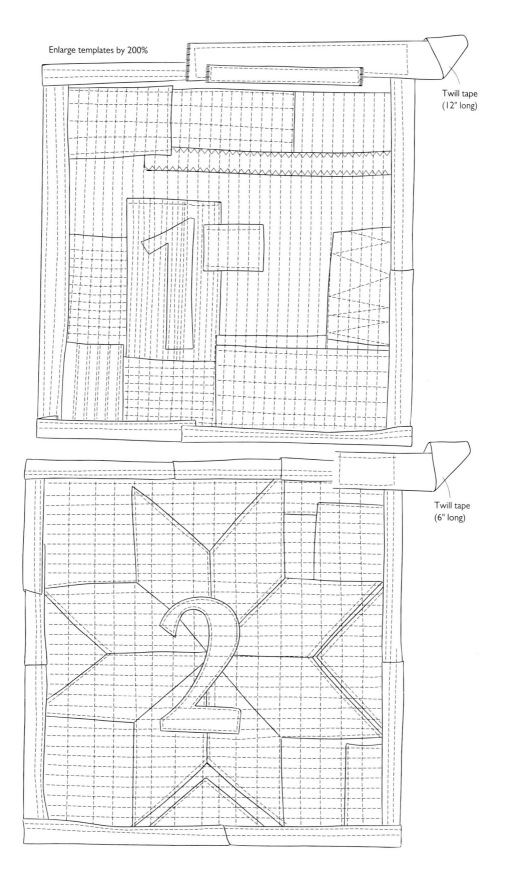

Enlarge templates by 200%

Twill tape
(12" long)

Twill tape
(6" long)

Appliquéd Room Shoes

{PHOTOGRAPH ON PAGE 18}

MATERIALS (MAKES 1 PAIR)

* Fabric for shoe top (linen): (2) 9¼" × 8"
* Fabric for appliqué (assorted prints): Scraps and sizes as desired
* Fabric for outside heel (striped): (2) 4½" × 4"
* Fabric for outside sole (dotted): (2) 4¼" × 10½"
* Fabric for the lining: (2) 9¼" × 8", (2) 4¼" × 10½"
* Quilt batting: (2) 9¼" × 8", (2) 4¼" × 10½"

INSTRUCTIONS

1. Roughly cut out the fabric for the top of each shoe, leaving a fairly large seam allowance. Following the instructions on page 56, machine appliqué the shoe tops as shown or as desired. Using the patterns on pages 70–71, cut the shoe tops and soles to size, leaving a seam allowance.

2. Lay the shoe tops and soles right side up on the quilt batting, and machine quilt the pieces together.

3. Using the pattern on page 71, cut out the heels to size. With right sides together, match corner a of one heel with corner a of one shoe top. Machine stitch the pieces, and press the seam allowance open. Repeat this process for the other side of the heel, matching corner b of the heel and corner b of the shoe top. Repeat for the other shoe. Using a running stitch (see page 63, hand stitch the toe of each shoe and use the thread to gather the fabric.

4. Place the right side of the shoe on the wrong side of the sole. Machine stitch around the shoe. Turn the piece right side out. Repeat this process for the other shoe. Sew the lining together following steps 1 to 4.

5. Place the lining in the shoe, right sides together. Sew around the opening of the shoe, leaving a gap. Cut slits in the fabric along the curve.

6. Turn the shoe right side out through the gap. Machine stitch around the opening, closing the gap.

7. Fold the heel down to the sole, and sew it in place.

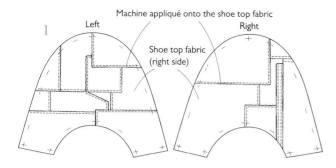

1   Left   Machine appliqué onto the shoe top fabric   Right

Shoe top fabric
(right side)

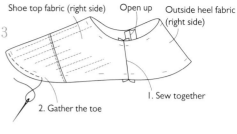

3   Shoe top fabric (right side)   Open up   Outside heel fabric (right side)

1. Sew together

2. Gather the toe

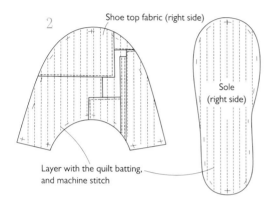

2

Shoe top fabric (right side)

Sole
(right side)

Layer with the quilt batting,
and machine stitch

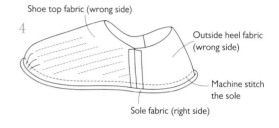

4

Shoe top fabric (wrong side)

Outside heel fabric
(wrong side)

Machine stitch
the sole

Sole fabric (right side)

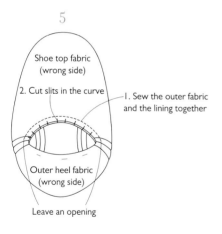

5

Shoe top fabric
(wrong side)

2. Cut slits in the curve

1. Sew the outer fabric
and the lining together

Outer heel fabric
(wrong side)

Leave an opening

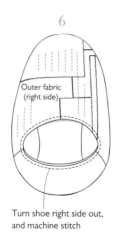

6

Outer fabric
(right side)

Turn shoe right side out,
and machine stitch

7

Fold the heel down to the sole,
and sew it in place

Appliquéd Floor Mat

}PHOTOGRAPH ON PAGE 19{

MATERIALS (makes 1)

* Fabric for the top (solid): (1) 27½" × 18¼"
* Fabric for the appliqué (assorted prints): Scraps and sizes as desired
* Fabric for the backing: (1) 27½" × 18¼"
* Quilt batting: (1) 27½" × 18¼"
* Fabric for the back (checkered): (1) 28⅞" × 19⅝"

INSTRUCTIONS

1. Following the instructions on page 56, machine appliqué the fabric scraps as shown or as desired onto the top fabric. Layer the backing, quilt batting, and fabric top, and machine quilt the entire piece.

2. With the back fabric wrong side up, fold in all four edges by ⅜". Mark a hemline 1" from the edge, and fold the corner up to meet the marked lines. Place the top fabric on the back fabric, wrong sides together. Fold the back fabric in along the hemline and over the top fabric. Machine stitch around the edge of the back fabric.

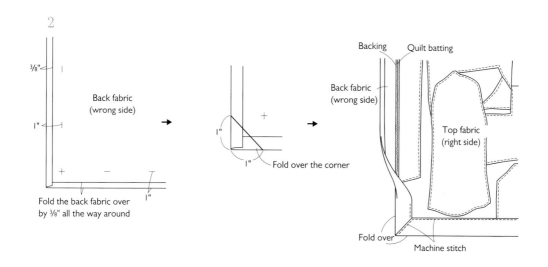

2

3/8"

Back fabric
(wrong side)

1"

1"

Fold the back fabric over
by 3/8" all the way around

1"

Fold over the corner

Backing   Quilt batting

Back fabric
(wrong side)

Top fabric
(right side)

Fold over

Machine stitch

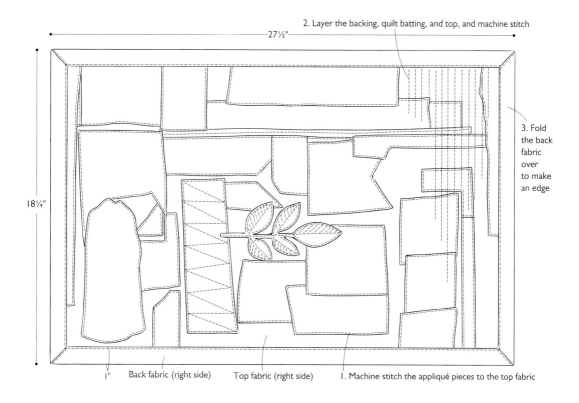

2. Layer the backing, quilt batting, and top, and machine stitch

←————————— 27½" —————————→

18¼"

3. Fold
the back
fabric
over
to make
an edge

1"   Back fabric (right side)   Top fabric (right side)   1. Machine stitch the appliqué pieces to the top fabric

Checkered Purse

❧ PHOTOGRAPH PAGE 23 ❧

MATERIALS (MAKES 1)

* Fabric for the purse top (wool): (2) 5⅛" × 3⅜"
* Fabric for the patchwork (assorted prints): (30) 1⅜" squares
* Fabric for the lining (striped): (2) 5⅛" × 6"
* Quilt batting: (2) 5⅛" × 6"
* Clasp (1)

INSTRUCTIONS

1. Following the instructions on pages 48–51, sew the patchwork pieces together to form the front of the purse. You will have five columns of three squares. Using the pattern on page 75, cut out the wool pieces for the purse top. Place the wool and patchwork right sides together and sew. Place the purse front on the quilt batting, and quilt along the seams. Repeat this step for the purse back.

2. Place the purse front and purse back right sides together. Stitch along three sides, leaving a gap at the top of the bag as shown. Repeat this step for the lining.

3. Turn the outer purse right side out. Fold the seam allowance around the top of the outer purse toward the wrong side. Fold the seam allowance of the lining toward the wrong side.

4. Place the lining in the purse, wrong sides together. Using a blind stitch (see page 63, sew the lining and purse together around the purse top. Using a running stitch (see page 63), sew along the top edge of the purse. Pull the threads to gather the fabric to the size appropriate for the clasp.

5. Attach the clasp by placing it over the top edge of the purse and sewing it in place.

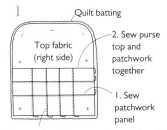

1
Quilt batting
Top fabric (right side)
2. Sew purse top and patchwork together
1. Sew patchwork panel
3. Layer with quilt batting, and quilt along the seams

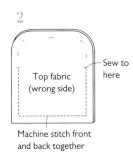

2
Top fabric (wrong side)
Sew to here
Machine stitch front and back together

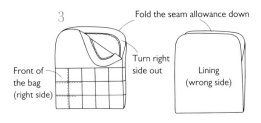

3
Fold the seam allowance down
Front of the bag (right side)
Turn right side out
Lining (wrong side)

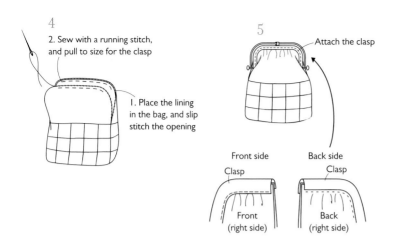

4

2. Sew with a running stitch, and pull to size for the clasp

1. Place the lining in the bag, and slip stitch the opening

5

Attach the clasp

Front side

Back side

Clasp

Clasp

Front
(right side)

Back
(right side)

Actual Size Pattern

Outer bag and lining (2 pieces each)

Purse top

Sew to here

Sew to here

Cut the patchwork pieces with a seam allowance of ¼";
cut the top fabric and lining with a seam allowance of ⅜"

Alphabet Pillow Cover

{PHOTOGRAPH PAGE 21}

MATERIALS (MAKES 1)

* Fabric for the pillow front (linen): For A–E: (2) 5½" × 4" and (2) 4" × 12½"; for K and R: (2) 6½" × 3½" and (2) 3½" × 12½"; for Z: (2) 6½" × 2½" and (2) 2½" × 10½"
* Fabric for the pillow back (linen): For A–E, K, and R: (1) 10¾" × 10¾"; for Z: (1) 12¾" × 12¾"
* Fabric for the patchwork (assorted prints and solids): Scraps and sizes vary per letter
* Fabric for the backing: For A–E, K, and R: (1) 10¾" × 10¾"; for Z: (1) 12¾" × 12¾"
* Pillow form: For A–E, K, and R: (1) 11" × 11"; for Z: (1) 9" × 9"

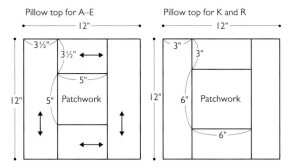

Pillow top for A–E

Pillow top for K and R

Patchwork

Cut with a seam allowance of ⅜"

INSTRUCTIONS

1. Following the patterns on pages 78–79, sew the patchwork center. Sew the front borders around the patchwork, first the top and bottom pieces, then the sides. Layer the backing, quilt batting, and pillow top, and machine quilt as shown on page 57.

2. Fold each panel for the back in half, and machine stitch ⅜" in from the folded edge. Layer the back panels on the pillow top, right sides together, making sure the folds of the back panel overlap near the center. Machine stitch around all four sides, then zigzag stitch along the edges to prevent fraying.

3. Turn the pillow cover right side out, and insert a pillow form.

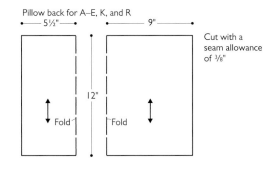

Pillow back for A–E, K, and R

Cut with a seam allowance of ⅜"

Fold

Fold

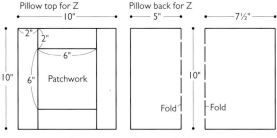

Pillow top for Z

Pillow back for Z

Patchwork

Fold

Fold

Cut with a seam allowance of ⅜"

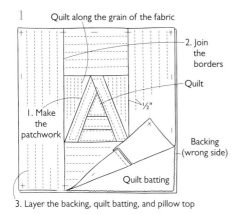

1

Quilt along the grain of the fabric

2. Join the borders

Quilt

½"

1. Make the patchwork

Backing (wrong side)

Quilt batting

3. Layer the backing, quilt batting, and pillow top

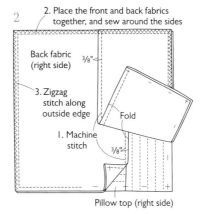

2

2. Place the front and back fabrics together, and sew around the sides

Back fabric (right side)

3/8"

3. Zigzag stitch along outside edge

Fold

1. Machine stitch

3/8"

Pillow top (right side)

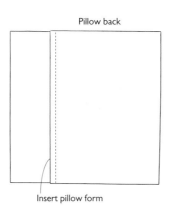

3

Pillow top

Pillow back

Insert pillow form

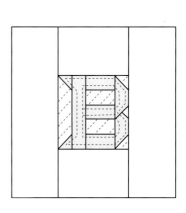

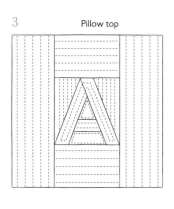

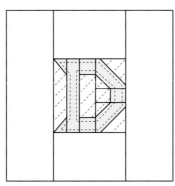

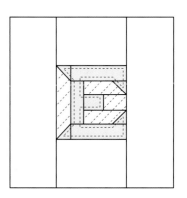

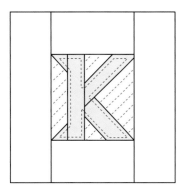
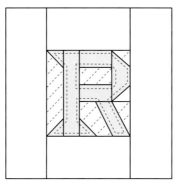
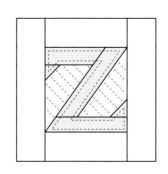

Patterns: Enlarge by 200%

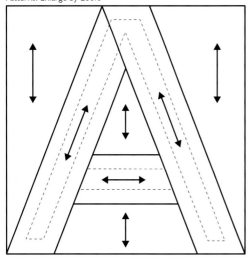
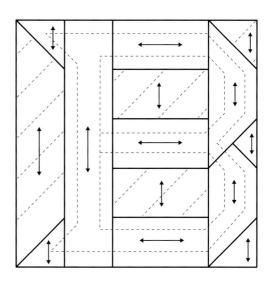

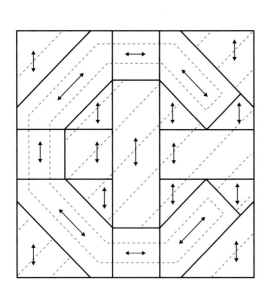
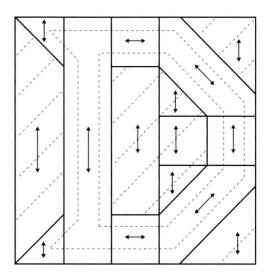

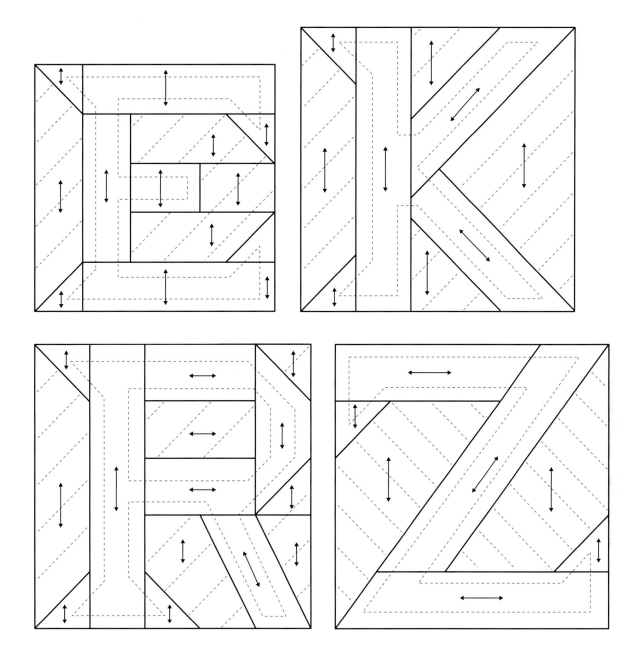

Star Flower Mini Pouch

{SEE PHOTOGRAPH PAGE 24}

Materials (makes 1)

* Fabric for the patchwork (assorted prints): Fabric a: (2) 5" × 2½"; fabric b: (1) ⅞" × ⅞"; fabric c: (4) 1" × 2⅝"
* Fabric for the backing: (1) 5¼" × 9¾"
* Fabric for the lining: (1) 5¼" × 9¾"
* Fabric for the bias binding: (1) ¾" × 9⅞"
* Quilt batting: (1) 5¼" × 9¾"
* Zipper: (1) 5¾" long
* Buttons: (4) ½" diameter (optional)

Instructions

1. Using the pattern to the right and following the diagrams, sew the patchwork panels for the pouch front and pouch back.
2. Place pouch front and pouch back right sides together, and sew along the bottom edge. Open the pouch front/back, and layer the backing, quilting batting, and patchwork. Machine quilt around the patchwork and in rows ½" apart.
3. Fold the patchwork along the seam, right sides together. Sew along both sides. Repeat this step for the lining fabric. Turn the patchwork right side out.
4. Place the lining in the patchwork pouch, wrong sides together. Following the instructions on pages 54–55, cover the opening of the pouch with bias binding, and sew it in place. Use a blind stitch (see page 63), to sew the binding to the inside of the pouch.
5. Place the zipper along the outside of the bag opening. Sew in place, aligning the edge of the zipper with the bias binding. Blind stitch the ends of the zipper together; attach buttons, if desired.

Pattern: Enlarge by 170%

Outside and lining (2 pieces each)

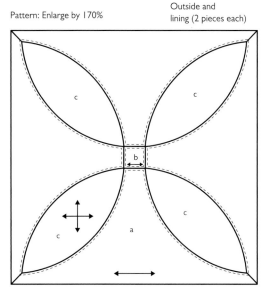

Cut the patchwork with a seam allowance of ¼"; cut the lining with a seam allowance of ⅜"

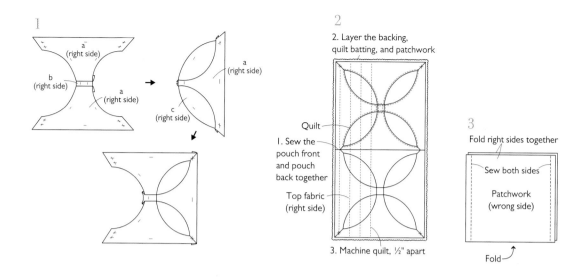

1

a (right side)

b (right side)

a (right side)

a (right side)

c (right side)

2

2. Layer the backing, quilt batting, and patchwork

Quilt

1. Sew the pouch front and pouch back together

Top fabric (right side)

3. Machine quilt, ½" apart

3

Fold right sides together

Sew both sides

Patchwork (wrong side)

Fold

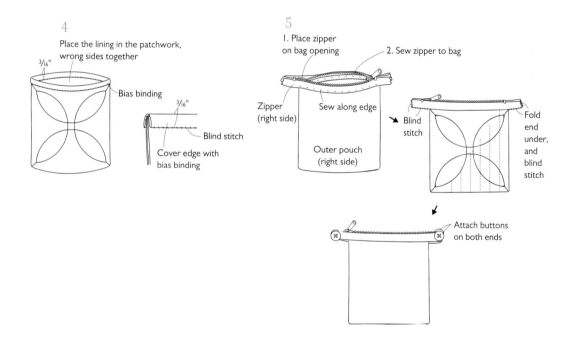

4

Place the lining in the patchwork, wrong sides together

³/₁₆"

Bias binding

³/₁₆"

Blind stitch

Cover edge with bias binding

5

1. Place zipper on bag opening

2. Sew zipper to bag

Zipper (right side)

Sew along edge

Outer pouch (right side)

Blind stitch

Fold end under, and blind stitch

Attach buttons on both ends

Log Cabin Mini Pouch

{SEE PHOTOGRAPH PAGE 24}

MATERIALS (MAKES 1)

* Fabric for the patchwork (assorted prints): Scraps and sizes as desired
* Fabric for the backing: (1) $4\frac{3}{4}$" × $8\frac{3}{4}$"
* Fabric for the lining: (1) $4\frac{3}{4}$" × $8\frac{3}{4}$"
* Fabric for the bias binding: (1) $\frac{3}{4}$" × $8\frac{3}{8}$"
* Quilt batting: (1) $4\frac{3}{4}$" × $8\frac{3}{4}$"
* Zipper: (1) 5" long
* Buttons: (4) $\frac{1}{2}$" diameter (optional)

INSTRUCTIONS

1. Using the pattern and following the instructions in the sidebar on page 83, sew the log cabin panels for the pouch front and pouch back.

2. To complete the pouch, follow steps 2 through 5 of the Star Flower Mini Pouch on page 80.

Actual Size Pattern

Outer pouch, lining (2 pieces each)

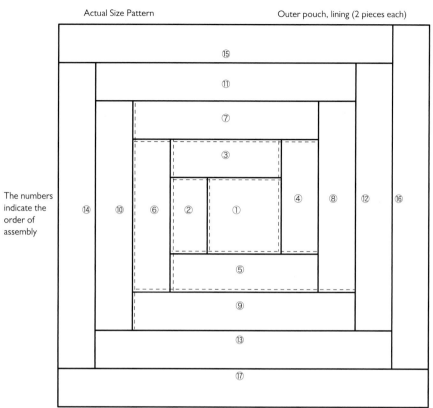

The numbers indicate the order of assembly

Cut the patchwork pieces with a seam allowance of ¼";
cut the lining with a seam allowance of ⅜"

HOW TO SEW THE LOG CABINS

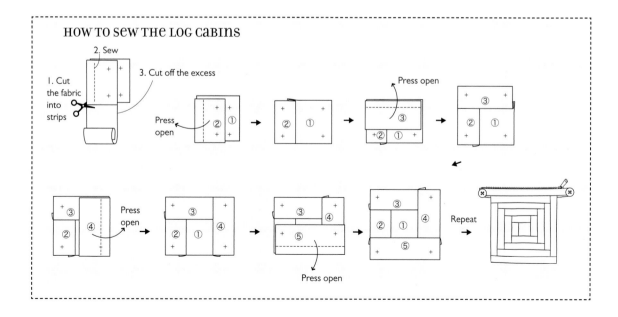

1. Cut the fabric into strips

2. Sew

3. Cut off the excess

Press open

Press open

Press open

Press open

Repeat

Checkered Shoulder Bag

{ S E E   P H O T O G R A P H   O N   P A G E   30 }

Materials (makes 1)

* Fabric for outer bag, patchwork, and gusset (fabric a, linen dots): (4) 3¾" × 3¼", (1) 10¼" × 3¼", (1) 13½" × 8¾", (1) 3½" × 38¼"
* Fabric for patchwork (fabric b, linen prints): (4) 3¾" × 3¼", (1) 3¾" × 2⅛", (1) 3¾" × 1⅝"
* Fabric for outer bag base (fabric c, satin): (2) 13½" × 4½"
* Fabric for the lining and gusset (striped): (2) 13¾" × 12¾", (1) 10¾" × 6¾", (1) 3½" × 38¼"
* Fabric for the backing: (2) 13½" × 12¾", (1) 3½" × 38¼"
* Quilt batting: (2) 13½" × 12¾", (1) 3½" × 38¼"
* Felt: (1) 8" × 4"
* Fusible interfacing: 6¾" × 5¾"
* Colored belt: 1" × 63"
* Buckle: 1 set
* D-ring: 2
* Magnetic snaps: 2 sets
* Embroidery floss: Small amount

Instructions

1. Following the instructions on pages 48–51, sew the patchwork pieces together to form the bag front. Using the pattern on page 87, cut the numbers from the felt. Attach the appliqué number to the bag front using the embroidery floss and a blanket stitch (see page 63). Layer the backing, quilt batting, and bag front. Mark the quilting lines, and machine quilt as shown.
2. Repeat step 1 for the bag back.
3. Layer the backing, quilt batting, and outer fabric for the gusset, and machine quilt.
4. Attached the fusible interfacing to half of the pocket fabric. Fold the pocket in half, and sew along all three sides, leaving a small gap. Turn the pocket right side out. Position the pocket on the right side of the lining, and sew in place.
5. Place the lining front and one piece of gusset lining right sides together, and sew along three sides. Place the lining back on the second piece of gusset lining, and sew along three sides, leaving a gap. Repeat this process for the quilted bag front, gusset, and bag back to form the outer bag; do not leave a gap when sewing the gusset to the outer bag.
6. Pass 2" of the colored belt through each of the D-rings. Baste the D-rings in place on the outer bag. Place the outer bag in the lining, right sides together, making sure the D-rings are between the outer bag and lining, and sew around the top edge, securing the D-rings in place. Turn the bag right side out through the gap in the lining, and sew the gap closed with a blind stitch (see page 63).

7. Topstitch around the opening of the bag. Secure the magnetic snaps in place. Run the buckle through the belt. Run one end of the belt through a D-ring, and sew it in place. Run the other end of the belt through the other D-ring and up through the back of the buckle; sew it in place.

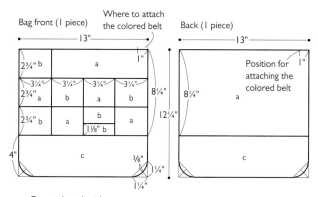

Bag front (1 piece)

Where to attach the colored belt

Back (1 piece)

Lining (2 pieces)

Cut patchwork with a seam allowance of ¼"; cut bag with a seam allowance of ⅜"

Cut with a seam allowance of ⅜"

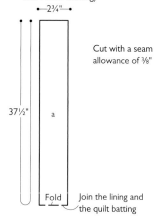

Gusset (1 from outer fabric, 1 from lining, 1 from batting, and 1 from backing)

Cut with a seam allowance of ⅜"

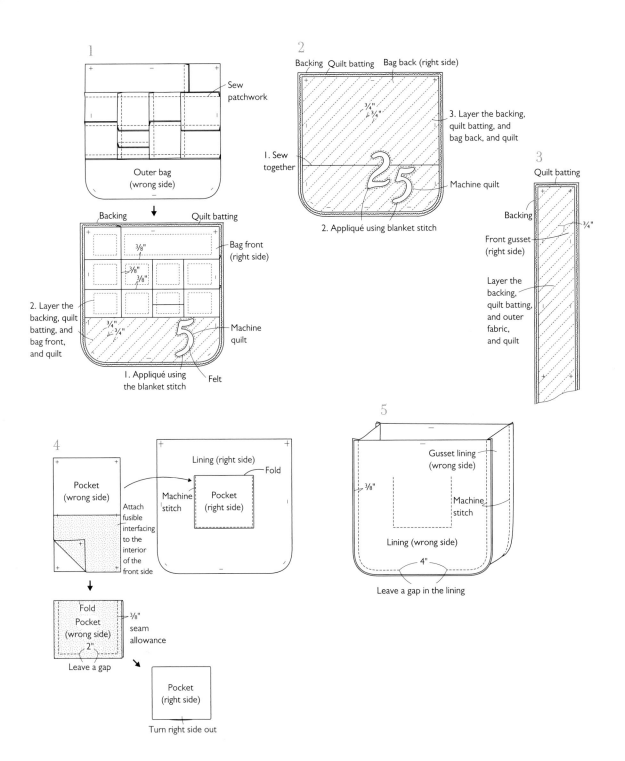

1

Sew patchwork

Outer bag (wrong side)

Backing Quilt batting

Bag front (right side)

2. Layer the backing, quilt batting, and bag front, and quilt

Machine quilt

3/8"

3/8"
3/8"

3/4"
3/4"

1. Appliqué using the blanket stitch

Felt

2

Backing Quilt batting Bag back (right side)

3. Layer the backing, quilt batting, and bag back, and quilt

3/4"
3/4"

1. Sew together

Machine quilt

2. Appliqué using blanket stitch

3

Quilt batting

Backing

Front gusset (right side)

3/4"

Layer the backing, quilt batting, and outer fabric, and quilt

4

Pocket (wrong side)

Attach fusible interfacing to the interior of the front side

Lining (right side)

Fold

Machine stitch

Pocket (right side)

Fold
Pocket (wrong side)

3/8"
seam allowance

2"

Leave a gap

Pocket (right side)

Turn right side out

5

Gusset lining (wrong side)

Machine stitch

3/8"

Lining (wrong side)

4"

Leave a gap in the lining

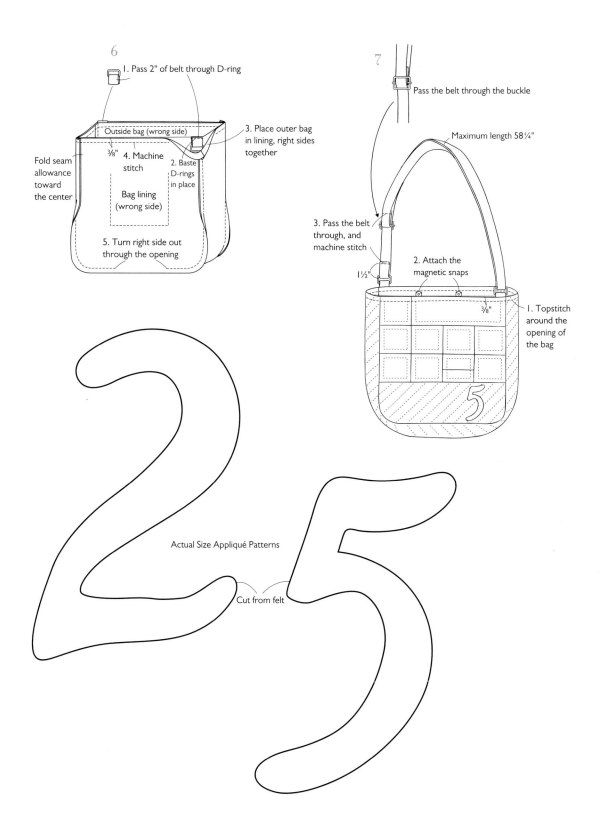

6

1. Pass 2" of belt through D-ring

Outside bag (wrong side)

3. Place outer bag in lining, right sides together

⅜" 4. Machine stitch

Fold seam allowance toward the center

2. Baste D-rings in place

Bag lining (wrong side)

5. Turn right side out through the opening

7

Pass the belt through the buckle

Maximum length 58¼"

3. Pass the belt through, and machine stitch

2. Attach the magnetic snaps

1½"

⅜"

1. Topstitch around the opening of the bag

Actual Size Appliqué Patterns

Cut from felt

Appliquéd Mini Bag

{SEE PHOTOGRAPH ON PAGE 29}

MATERIALS (MAKES 1)

* Fabric for the outer bag (fabric a, linen dots): (2) $5\frac{1}{2}$" × $3\frac{1}{8}$"
* Fabric for the outer bag (fabric b, satin): (2) $5\frac{1}{2}$" × $5\frac{3}{8}$"
* Fabric for the lining (stripes): (2) $5\frac{1}{2}$" × $7\frac{3}{4}$"
* Fabric for the gusset (fabric b and lining): (2) $1\frac{7}{8}$" × $10\frac{1}{8}$" each
* Fabric for the bias binding (fabric a): (1) 1" × $9\frac{1}{2}$"
* Fabric for the bias binding (fabric b): (2) 1" × $36\frac{3}{4}$"
* Quilt batting: (2) $5\frac{1}{2}$" × $7\frac{3}{4}$", (1) $1\frac{7}{8}$" × $19\frac{1}{2}$"
* Felt: (1) $2\frac{3}{8}$" × 4"
* Leather strap for the handles: (2) $\frac{1}{8}$" × $15\frac{3}{4}$"

INSTRUCTIONS

1. Using the pattern on page 87, cut the number from felt. Attach the appliqué number to the bottom of the bag front. Place the bottom of the bag front and the top of the bag front right sides together and sew. Layer the lining, quilt batting, and bag front. Baste around the number and along the seam, and machine quilt as shown.
2. Repeat step 1 for the bag back.
3. Place the two outside gusset pieces right sides together, and sew along one short edge. Repeat this step for the lining gusset. Press the outside gusset open, and layer the lining, quilt batting, and outer

fabric. Machine quilt two rows down the length of the gusset.
4. Place the bag front and gusset wrong sides together, and sew along three sides. Repeat this step for the bag back. Trim the outside seam allowance to $\frac{1}{4}$".
5. Following the instructions on pages 54–55, cover the seam allowances with bias binding. Fold the seam allowance over, and sew it in place with a blind stitch.
6. Cover the opening of the bag with bias binding, and sew in place. Use a blind stitch to sew the binding to the inside of the bag. Sew the straps in place along the quilted lines.

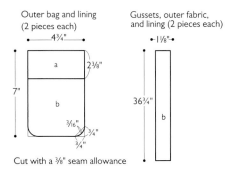

Outer bag and lining (2 pieces each)

Gussets, outer fabric, and lining (2 pieces each)

Cut with a $\frac{3}{8}$" seam allowance

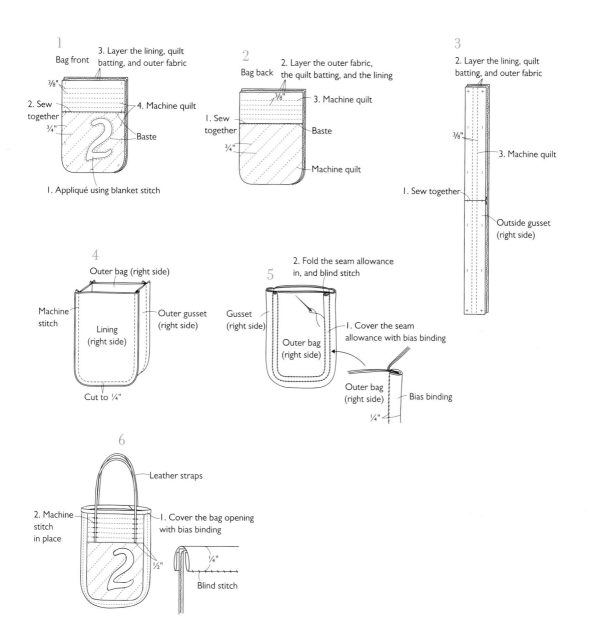

1

Bag front

3. Layer the lining, quilt batting, and outer fabric

3/8"

2. Sew together

3/4"

4. Machine quilt

Baste

1. Appliqué using blanket stitch

2

Bag back

2. Layer the outer fabric, the quilt batting, and the lining

3/8"

3. Machine quilt

1. Sew together

3/4"

Baste

Machine quilt

3

2. Layer the lining, quilt batting, and outer fabric

3/8"

3. Machine quilt

1. Sew together

Outside gusset (right side)

4

Outer bag (right side)

Machine stitch

Lining (right side)

Outer gusset (right side)

Cut to 1/4"

5

2. Fold the seam allowance in, and blind stitch

Gusset (right side)

Outer bag (right side)

1. Cover the seam allowance with bias binding

Outer bag (right side)

Bias binding

1/4"

6

Leather straps

2. Machine stitch in place

1. Cover the bag opening with bias binding

1/2"

1/4"

Blind stitch

89

Pleated Shoulder Bag

⁂{ S EE PHOTOGRAPH ON PAGE 31 }⁂

MATERIALS (MAKES 1)

* Fabric for outer bag (fabric a, synthetic leather): (2) 5¾" × 9¾"
* Fabric for patchwork (fabric b, print): (3) 2¾" × 8¼"
* Fabric for patchwork (fabric c, striped): (2) 2¾" × 8¼"
* Fabric for gusset (fabric a and lining): (2) 4" × 14¾" each
* Fabric for the lining (print): (2) 18¾" × 9¾"
* Fabric for zipper binding: (4) 2¼" × 3½"
* Fabric for backing: (2) 18¾" × 9¾"
* Quilt batting: (2) 18¾" × 9¾", (1) 4" × 28¾"
* Leather strip for handle: (2) ⅜" × 25"
* Zipper: (1) 22¾" long

INSTRUCTIONS

1. Following the instructions on pages 48–51 and referring to the pattern on page 93 and the diagram, sew the patchwork pieces together to form the bag front. Layer the backing, quilt batting, and bag front. Machine quilt as shown in the center patchwork section. Sew around the edge of the bag. Repeat the process for the bag back.

2. Make two pleats on the bag front and bag back by folding fabric c over on itself so that the corners of fabric b on each side meet in the middle front of fabric c. Make sure the machine stitching along the bag edge aligns across the pleat. Baste in place.

3. Place the two outside gusset pieces right sides together, and sew along one edge. Repeat this step for the backing. Press open, and layer the backing, quilt batting, and outer fabric. Stitch around the edge of the gusset.

4. Place the bag front and gusset wrong sides together, and sew along three sides. Repeat this step for the bag back. Fold the seam allowance toward the gusset, and fold the top edge of the gusset under by ⅜". Sew the ends of two leather straps to each side of the bag along the top of the gusset.

5. Place two pieces of the zipper binding fabric right sides together, and sew along three sides. Cut the slit, and fold back the seam allowance as shown. Turn the binding right side out. Place the binding over one end of the zipper, and sew in place. Repeat this process for the second binding. Place the zipper in the bag opening with the right side of the zipper against the wrong side of the bag. Sew the zipper in place around the opening of the bag. Trim the seam allowance from the fabrics, and quilt batting closely. Turn the bag wrong side out.

6. Sew the lining as for the outer bag, making pleats in the same positions.

7. Place the lining over the bag, wrong sides together. Hand sew the lining to zipper using a blind stitch.

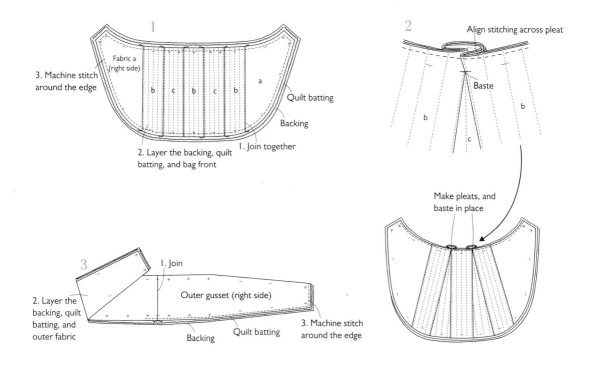

1

3. Machine stitch around the edge

Fabric a (right side)

Quilt batting

Backing

b c b c b

a

2. Layer the backing, quilt batting, and bag front

1. Join together

2

Align stitching across pleat

Baste

b

b

c

Make pleats, and baste in place

3

1. Join

2. Layer the backing, quilt batting, and outer fabric

Outer gusset (right side)

3. Machine stitch around the edge

Backing

Quilt batting

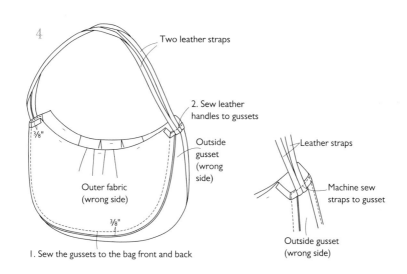

4

Two leather straps

2. Sew leather handles to gussets

Outside gusset (wrong side)

3/8"

Outer fabric (wrong side)

3/8"

1. Sew the gussets to the bag front and back

Leather straps

Machine sew straps to gusset

Outside gusset (wrong side)

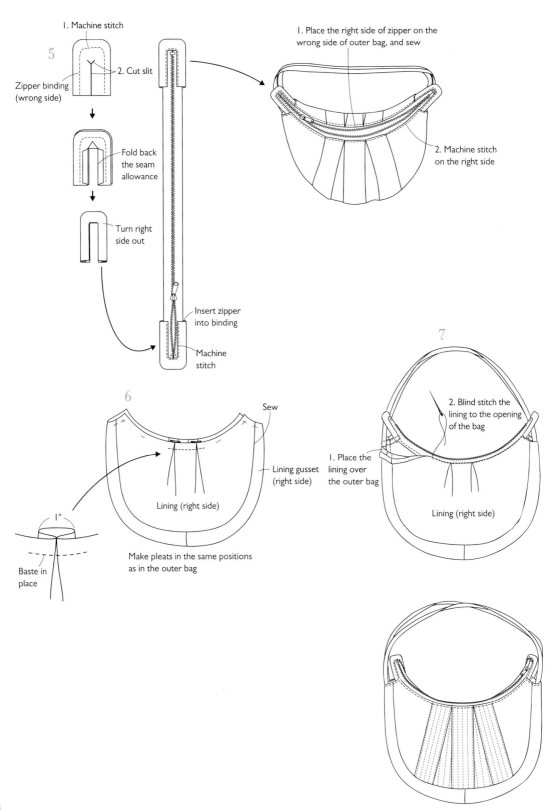

5

1. Machine stitch

2. Cut slit

Zipper binding (wrong side)

Fold back the seam allowance

Turn right side out

Insert zipper into binding

Machine stitch

1. Place the right side of zipper on the wrong side of outer bag, and sew

2. Machine stitch on the right side

7

2. Blind stitch the lining to the opening of the bag

1. Place the lining over the outer bag

Lining (right side)

6

Sew

Lining gusset (right side)

Lining (right side)

1"

Baste in place

Make pleats in the same positions as in the outer bag

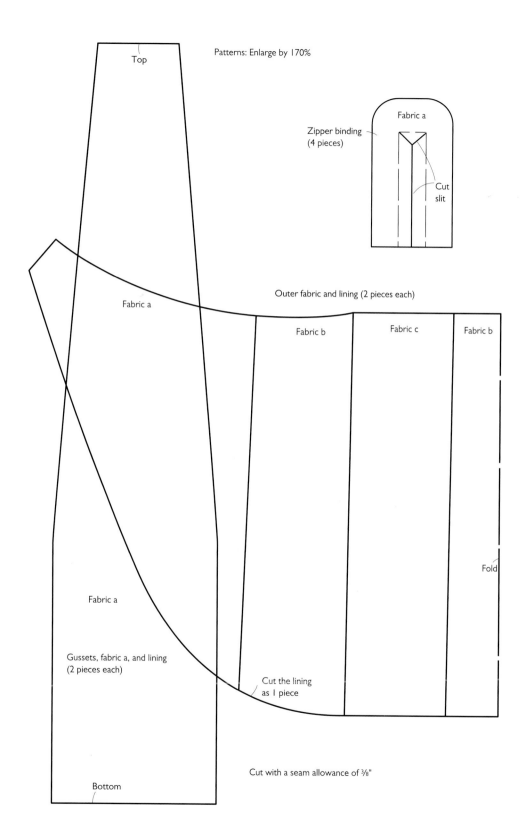

Top

Patterns: Enlarge by 170%

Fabric a

Zipper binding
(4 pieces)

Cut
slit

Outer fabric and lining (2 pieces each)

Fabric a

Fabric b

Fabric c

Fabric b

Fold

Fabric a

Gussets, fabric a, and lining
(2 pieces each)

Cut the lining
as 1 piece

Cut with a seam allowance of ⅜"

Bottom

93

Courthouse Steps Sewing Bag

{ SEE PHOTOGRAPH ON PAGE 32 }

MATERIALS (MAKES 1)

* Fabric for patchwork (fabric a, satin; fabric b and c, assorted prints): Strips of fabric ⅞" wide in varying lengths
* Fabric for gusset (fabric a and lining fabric): (1) 10¾" × 1⅞", (2) ⅞" × 20¾"
* Fabric for the lining (print): (2) 11¾" × 4¾"
* Fabric for the pockets (lining fabric): (2) 11¾" × 6¼"
* Fabric for the handles (fabric a): (2) 8⅝" × 1½"
* Fabric for the bias binding (lining fabric): (1) 1" × 30⅜"
* Fabric for the backing: (2) 11¾" × 4¾", (1) 10¾" × 1⅞", (2) ⅞" × 20¾"
* Quilt batting: (2) 11¾" × 4¾", (1) 10¾" × 1⅞", (2) ⅞" × 20¾"
* Zipper: (1) 19" long

INSTRUCTIONS

1. Prepare two handles by folding the long edges in to the center, then folding the fabric in half. Stitch along the long edge.
2. Referring to the pattern on page 95 and following the sidebar on page 123, make four courthouse steps for the bag front. Sew the four patchwork pieces together as shown. Layer the backing, quilt batting, and patchwork, and trim the bag front to size. Machine quilt along the seams. Prepare the lining by sewing on the pockets. Place the lining on the bag front, wrong sides together, and baste along the edge on all four sides. Baste the handle to the right side of the bag front. Repeat this process for the bag back.
3. Referring to the diagram on page 95 and following the instructions on page 122, sew the gusset together with the zipper.
4. Place the bag front and gusset wrong sides together, and sew along four sides. Repeat this step for the bag back. Following the instructions on pages 54–55, cover the seam allowances with bias binding. Fold the seam allowance under, and sew it to the lining with a blind stitch. Turn the bag right side out.

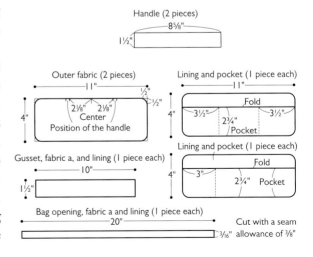

Handle (2 pieces)
8⅝"
1½"

Outer fabric (2 pieces)
11"
2⅛" 2⅛"
Center
Position of the handle
½"
½"
4"

Lining and pocket (1 piece each)
11"
Fold
3½" 3½"
2¾"
Pocket
4"

Gusset, fabric a, and lining (1 piece each)
10"
1½"

Lining and pocket (1 piece each)
Fold
3"
2¾" Pocket
4"

Bag opening, fabric a and lining (1 piece each)
20"
Cut with a seam
³⁄₁₆" allowance of ⅜"

Actual Size Pattern   **Make 8 patchwork pieces**

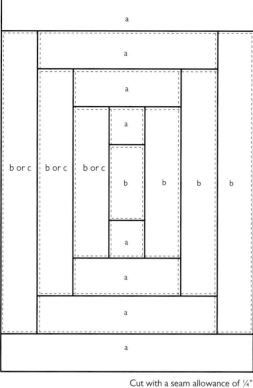

a

a

a

a

b or c | b or c | b or c | b | b | b | b

a

a

a

a

Cut with a seam allowance of ¼"

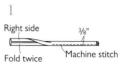

1

Right side   ³⁄₈"

Fold twice   Machine stitch

2

4. Baste lining to outer bag

5. Make the handle, and baste in place

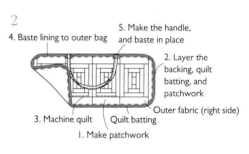

2. Layer the backing, quilt batting, and patchwork

Outer fabric (right side)

3. Machine quilt   Quilt batting

1. Make patchwork

3

Attach the zipper, and make a gusset   Zipper

Outer opening fabric (right side)

Lining opening fabric (right side)

Baste around the edge

Quilt batting

Gusset lining (right side)

Outer gusset (right side)

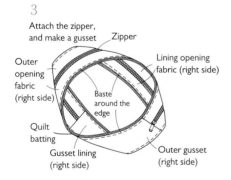

4

Lining (right side)   ³⁄₈"

1. Sew the gussets to the outer bag

3. Fold the allowance over toward the center and hem

2. Cover the seam allowance with the bias binding

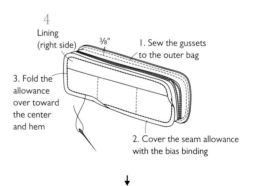

↓

95

Yo-Yo Glasses Case

∗{S EE PHOTOGRAPH ON PAGE 33}∗

MATERIALS (MAKES 1)

* Fabric for outer case (felt): (2) 7" × 7"
* Fabric for yo-yos b, c (assorted prints): Scraps and sizes as desired
* Fabric for the lining (print): (1) 7½" × 7½"

INSTRUCTIONS

1. Using the patterns below and following the diagrams on page 97, make the yo-yos for the case front.
2. Fold the edge of the lining fabric over by ¼". Place the lining on one piece of felt, wrong sides together, making sure the curved edge is on the right.
3. Take the second piece of felt, and sew the yo-yos to the right side in a pleasing design, making sure the curved edge is on the left.
4. Place the two felt pieces together, felt side to felt side. Fold the case in half, and use a blind stitch to sew along the side and bottom.

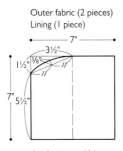

Outer fabric (2 pieces)
Lining (1 piece)

7"
3½"
1½" ³⁄₈"
7" 5½"

Cut 2 pieces of felt with no seam allowance; cut the lining with a seam allowance of ¼"

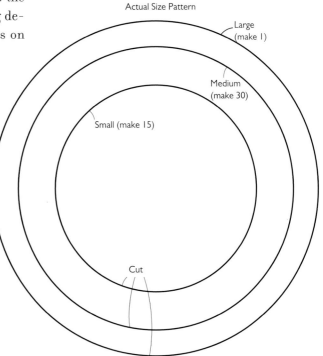

Actual Size Pattern

Large (make 1)

Medium (make 30)

Small (make 15)

Cut

1

Make the yo-yos

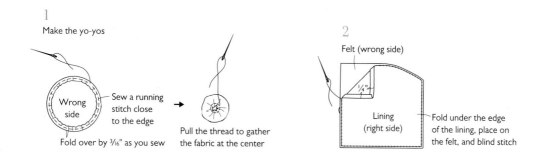

Wrong side

Sew a running
stitch close
to the edge

Fold over by ³/₁₆" as you sew

Pull the thread to gather
the fabric at the center

2

Felt (wrong side)

¹/₄"

Lining
(right side)

Fold under the edge
of the lining, place on
the felt, and blind stitch

3

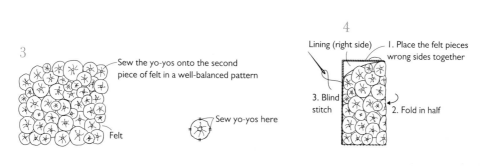

Sew the yo-yos onto the second
piece of felt in a well-balanced pattern

Felt

Sew yo-yos here

4

Lining (right side)

1. Place the felt pieces
wrong sides together

3. Blind
stitch

2. Fold in half

Tea Towel Tote Bag

❧ SEE PHOTOGRAPH ON PAGE 34 ❧

MATERIALS (MAKES 1)

* Fabric for the bag and handles: (1) tea towel about 19½" × 18" cut to the measurements shown
* Fabric for the appliqué (assorted prints): Scraps and sizes as desired

INSTRUCTIONS

1. Cut the bag fabric using the selvage of the tea towel for the opening of the bag. Following the instructions on page 56, appliqué the scraps of fabric as shown or as desired. Fold the fabric in half and, following the sidebar on page 99, sew a French seam along the bottom and side of the bag.
2. Prepare two handles by folding the long edges in to the center, and then folding the fabric in half. Stitch along the long edge.
3. Sew one handle to the bag front and one handle to the bag back, as shown.

Cut from one tea towel

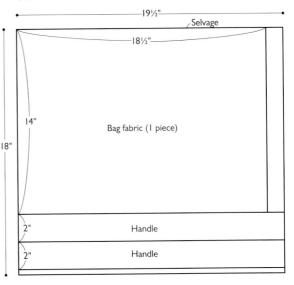

19½"

Selvage

18½"

14"

18"

Bag fabric (1 piece)

2" Handle

2" Handle

Use the selvage of the fabric for the bag opening   Machine appliqué

Handle

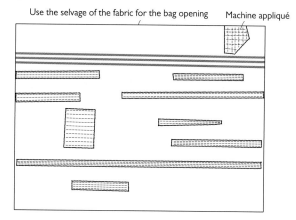

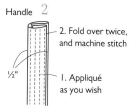

2. Fold over twice, and machine stitch

½"

1. Appliqué as you wish

3

2¾"

Handle

French seam

Machine stitch

2"

Bag fabric (wrong side)

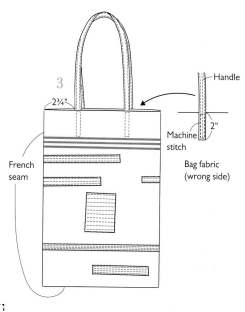

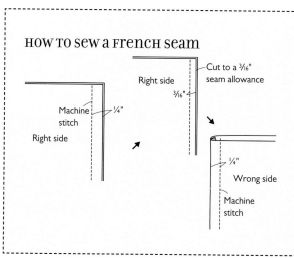

HOW TO SEW A FRENCH SEAM

Right side

Cut to a ³⁄₁₆" seam allowance

³⁄₁₆"

Machine stitch   ¼"

Right side

¼"

Wrong side

Machine stitch

Appliquéd Tote Bag

⟨SEE PHOTOGRAPH ON PAGE 35⟩

MATERIALS (MAKES 1)

* Fabric for the outer bag and handles (stripes): (1) 15¾" × 10¾", (2) 1½" × 13½"
* Fabric for the appliqué (assorted prints): Scraps and sizes as desired
* Fabric for the lining (print): (1) 15¾" × 10¾"
* Fabric for the backing: (1) 15¾" × 10¾"
* Quilt batting: (1) 15¾" × 10¾"

INSTRUCTIONS

1. Layer the backing, quilt batting, and outer bag fabric. Following the instructions on page 56, machine appliqué the scraps as shown or as desired, and machine quilt.

2. Fold the outer bag in half, right sides together. Machine stitch along the side and bottom; do not stitch along the cut-out corners. Open the seams, and flatten the bag bottom so that the raw edges along the bottom and side align; sew (see pages 120–121). Repeat this process for the lining, leaving a gap in the bottom seam.

3. Turn the bag right side out. Prepare two handles by folding the long edges in to the center, then folding the fabric in half. Stitch along the long edge. Baste the handles to the right side of the outer bag. Place the lining over the bag, right sides together, and sew around the bag opening. Turn the bag right side out through the gap in the lining. Sew the gap closed with a blind stitch.

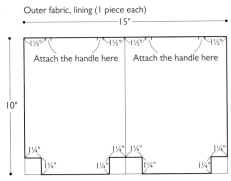

Outer fabric, lining (1 piece each)

15"

1½" · 1½" · 1½" · 1½"

Attach the handle here · Attach the handle here

10"

1¼" · 1¼" · 1¼" · 1¼"

1¼" · 1¼" · 1¼" · 1¼"

Cut with a seam allowance of ⅜"

Handle
(2 pieces)

1½"

13½"

Cut

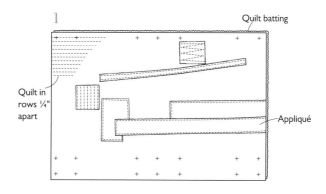

1

Quilt batting

Quilt in
rows ¼"
apart

Appliqué

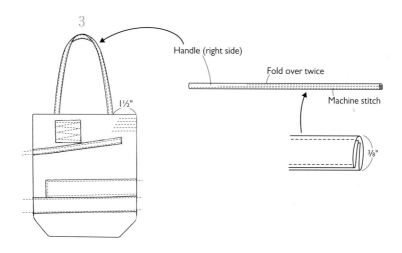

3

1½"

Handle (right side)

Fold over twice

Machine stitch

⅜"

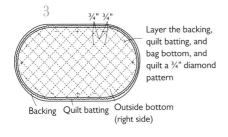

3

¾" ¾"

Layer the backing, quilt batting, and bag bottom, and quilt a ¾" diamond pattern

Backing Quilt batting Outside bottom (right side)

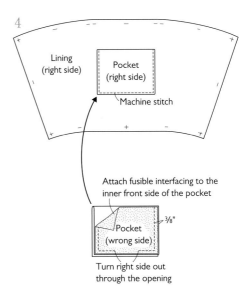

4

Lining (right side)

Pocket (right side)

Machine stitch

Attach fusible interfacing to the inner front side of the pocket

Pocket (wrong side)

⅜"

Turn right side out through the opening

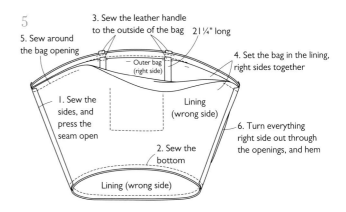

5

3. Sew the leather handle to the outside of the bag

21¼" long

5. Sew around the bag opening

Outer bag (right side)

4. Set the bag in the lining, right sides together

1. Sew the sides, and press the seam open

Lining (wrong side)

6. Turn everything right side out through the openings, and hem

2. Sew the bottom

Lining (wrong side)

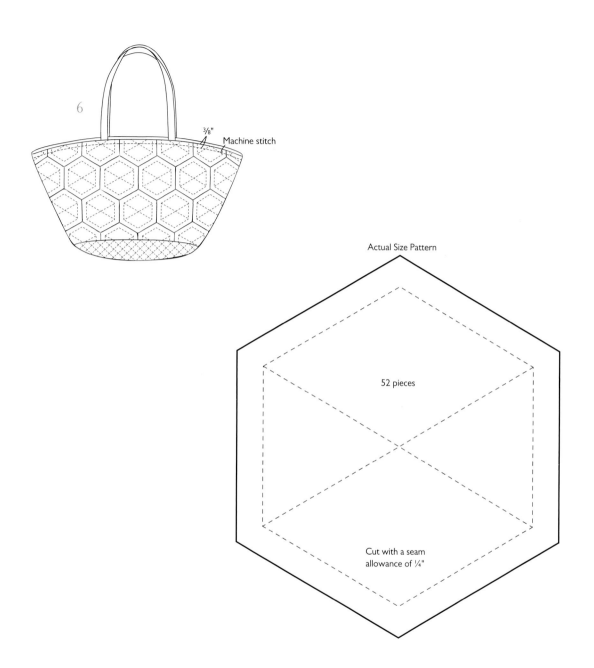

6

$\frac{3}{8}$"

Machine stitch

Actual Size Pattern

52 pieces

Cut with a seam
allowance of $\frac{1}{4}$"

Yo-Yo Bag

⟨SEE PHOTOGRAPH ON PAGE 38⟩

MATERIALS (MAKES 1)

* Fabric for outer bag, lining, pocket, and handle (gingham): (2) 9¾" × 9¾", (2) 9¾" × 9⅝", (1) 6¾" × 9¾", (1) 1½" × 14"
* Fabric for yo-yos (gingham and plain): (58) 3½" × 3½"
* Lace flowers: (14) 2" in diameter
* Fusible interfacing: (1) 6¾" × 5", (1) 1½" × 14"

INSTRUCTIONS

1. Attach the fusible interfacing to half of the pocket fabric. Fold the pocket in half, right sides together, and sew along all three sides, leaving a small gap. Turn the pocket right side out. Position the pocket on the right side of the lining, and sew it in place.

2. Attach the fusible interfacing to the wrong side of the handle fabric. Fold the long edges of each handle in to the center, then fold the fabric in half. Stitch along the long edge on both sides. Baste the handles to the right side of the outer bag.

3. Place the lining and the bag front right sides together. Sew along the top of the bag, securing the handle in place. Press the seams open, and lay the fabric flat.

Repeat this process for the bag back.

4. Place the bag front and lining on the bag back and lining, right sides together. Make sure the pieces are oriented so the outer fabric of the bag front is on the outer fabric of the bag back, and the lining front is on the lining back. Sew around all four edges, leaving a gap.

5. Turn the bag right side out, and sew the gap closed with a blind stitch. Tuck the lining inside the bag.

6. Using the template on page 107 and following the instructions on page 97, make the yo-yos. Sew the yo-yos and flowers together to form a rectangle of fabric made up of twelve yo-yos/flowers across and six down. Fold this fabric in half, wrong sides together, and sew along the side and bottom following the diagram.

7. Slip the yo-yo fabric over the bag. Sew the yo-yo fabric to the bag along the sides and bottom where indicated to secure in place.

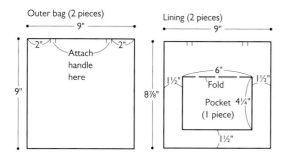

Outer bag (2 pieces)
9"

2" Attach handle here 2"

9"

Lining (2 pieces)
9"

8⅞"

1½" 6" 1½"
Fold
Pocket 4¼"
(1 piece)

1½"

Handle (2 pieces)
13¼"

1½" Cut

Cut with seam allowance of ⅜"

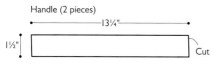

1

Pocket
(wrong side)

Attach fusible interfacing
to the wrong side of the
pocket front

↓

Pocket
(wrong side)

⅜"
Machine stitch

Turn right side out
through the opening

↓

Lining (right side) Fold

Pocket
(right side)

Machine stitch

Actual Size Pattern

Cut

58 pieces

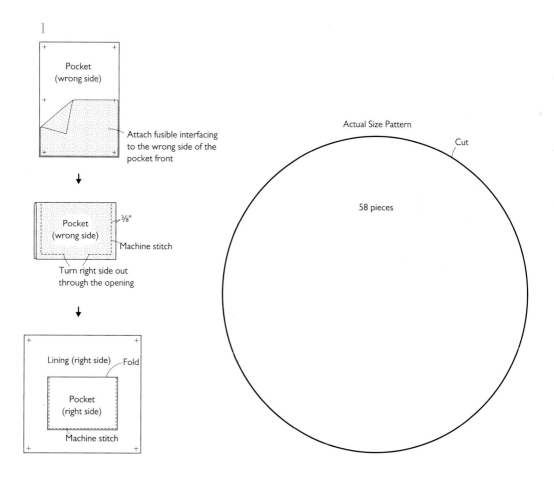

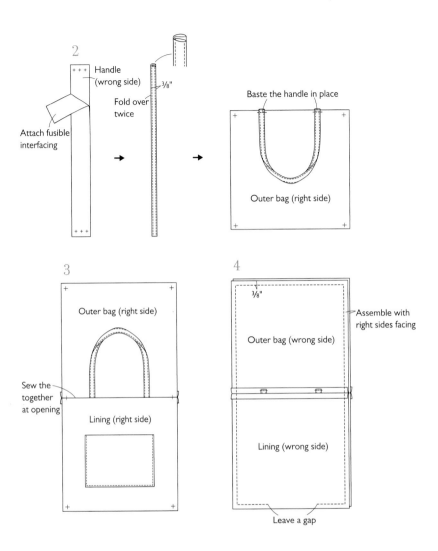

2

Handle (wrong side)

+ + +

Attach fusible interfacing

+ + +

Fold over twice

³⁄₈"

Baste the handle in place

Outer bag (right side)

3

Outer bag (right side)

Sew the together at opening

Lining (right side)

4

³⁄₈"

Assemble with right sides facing

Outer bag (wrong side)

Lining (wrong side)

Leave a gap

5   Turn the bag right side out,
    and blind stitch the gap

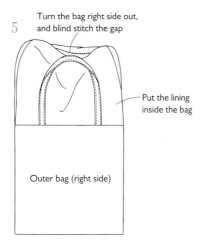

Put the lining
inside the bag

Outer bag (right side)

6

1. Sew the yo-yos and the flowers together

a   a
b   b
2. Fold in half;   c   c   Sew in place
sew sides together   d   d
at the corresponding   e   e
letters   f   f

    g   h   i   j   k   l   l   k   j   i   h   g

3. Sew bottom together at the corresponding letters

7

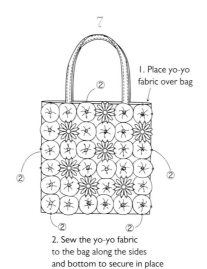

1. Place yo-yo
fabric over bag

②

②   ②

②   ②

2. Sew the yo-yo fabric
to the bag along the sides
and bottom to secure in place

Appliquéd Flat Bag

{SEE PHOTOGRAPH ON PAGE 37}

MATERIALS (MAKES 1)

* Fabric for bag front (fabric a, plain): (1) 14¼" × 7", (1) 14¼" × 3¾"
* Fabric for bag front, bag back, and handles (fabric b, print): (1) 14¼" × 4½", (1) 14¼" × 13¾", (2) 2" × 9¼"
* Fabric for appliqué: Scraps and sizes as desired
* Fabric for lining and pocket (print): (2) 14¼" × 13¾", (1) 7¾" × 11¾"
* Fabric for backing: (2) 14¼" × 13¾"
* Quilt batting: (2) 14¼" × 13¾"
* Fusible interfacing: (1) 7¾" × 6¼"

INSTRUCTIONS

1. Following the instructions on pages 48–51, sew the patchwork strips together to form the bag front. Following the instructions on page 56, attach the appliqué scraps to the bag front as shown or as desired. Layer the backing, quilt batting, and bag front. Mark the quilting lines, and machine quilt as shown. Repeat this process for the bag back.

2. Layer the quilt batting and handle fabric. Appliqué and quilt one handle as shown. Fold the long edges of each handle in by ⅜", and fold the fabric in half. Stitch along the long edge. Baste the handles to the right side of the outer bag.

3. Attach the fusible interfacing to half of the pocket fabric. Fold the pocket in half, right sides together, and sew along all three sides, leaving a small gap. Turn the pocket right side out. Position the pocket on the right side of the lining, and sew in place. (See page 107 for diagrams.)

4. Follow steps 3 through 5 on page 106 to sew the lining and bag together.

Bag front is patchwork;
bag back is one piece

Lining (2 pieces)

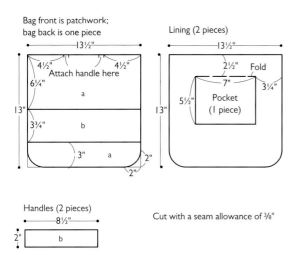

13½"

4½"   4½"
Attach handle here
6¼"
a
13"
3¾"   b

3"   a   2"
2"

13½"

2½"   Fold
7"
3¼"
5½"   Pocket
(1 piece)
13"

Handles (2 pieces)

8½"

2"   b

Cut with a seam allowance of ⅜"

1

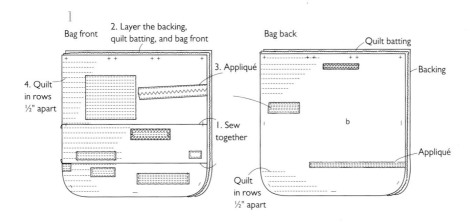

Bag front   2. Layer the backing,
quilt batting, and bag front

Bag back   Quilt batting

3. Appliqué

4. Quilt
in rows
½" apart

Backing

1. Sew
together

b

Appliqué

Quilt
in rows
½" apart

2

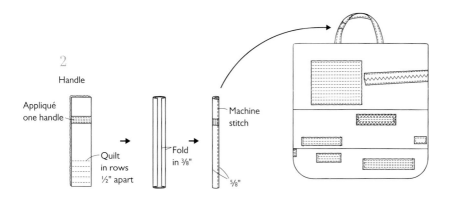

Handle

Appliqué
one handle

Quilt
in rows
½" apart

Fold
in ⅜"

Machine
stitch

⅝"

Hexagon Patchwork Book Cover

}See photograph on page 39{

Materials (makes 1)

* Fabric for patchwork (assorted prints): (148) $1^3/8$" × $1^1/2$"
* Fabric for lining, flap, and strap (striped): (1) $19^1/2$" × $7^5/8$", (1) $3^1/2$" × $7^5/8$", (1) $2^7/8$" × $8^3/8$"
* Fabric for backing: (1) $10^1/4$" × $7^5/8$"
* Quilt batting: (1) $10^1/4$" × $7^5/8$"
* Fusible interfacing: (1) $19^1/2$" × $7^5/8$", (1) $3^1/2$" × $7^5/8$"
* Ribbon: (1) $3/8$Đ × $26^1/4$", (1) $3/8$" × $9^1/4$"

Instructions

1. Using the pattern below and following the instructions on pages 48–51, sew the patchwork pieces together to form the book cover front. Layer the backing, quilt batting, and bag front. Mark the quilting lines, and machine quilt as shown.

2. Attach the fusible interfacing to the wrong side of the lining and flap. Place the patchwork fabric on the lining, right sides together, and sew along one side. Press open. Center the longer piece of ribbon on the side of the patchwork. Place the flap on the patchwork, right sides together, and sew along one side, securing the ribbon in place. Press open.

3. Fold the book cover in half, wrong sides together. Machine stitch along the fold.

4. Open the cover, and fold it in half, right sides together. Fold in the side pocket $3^1/4$". Make the fabric strap by folding the fabric in half, right sides together, and sewing down the long edge. Turn the fabric right side out, and press the seam allowance open. Sew along both sides. Insert the strap (the shorter piece of ribbon) in the book cover fabric, referring to the diagram for positioning. Sew along three sides, leaving a gap in the flap.

5. Turn the book cover right side out. Topstitch around the edge of the book cover, closing the gap. The finished inside of the book cover.

6. The finished outside of the book cover.

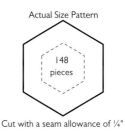

Actual Size Pattern

148 pieces

Cut with a seam allowance of $1/4$"

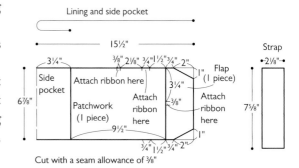

Lining and side pocket

$15^1/2$"

$3/8$" $2^1/8$" $3/4$" $1^1/2$" $3/4$" 2"

$3^1/4$"

Side pocket

Attach ribbon here

$3^1/4$"

Attach ribbon here

1"

Flap (1 piece)

$6^7/8$"

Patchwork (1 piece)

Attach ribbon here

$3/8$"

Attach ribbon here

$7^5/8$"

Strap

$2^1/8$"

$9^1/2$"

1"

$3/4$" $1^1/2$" $3/4$" 2"

Cut with a seam allowance of $3/8$"

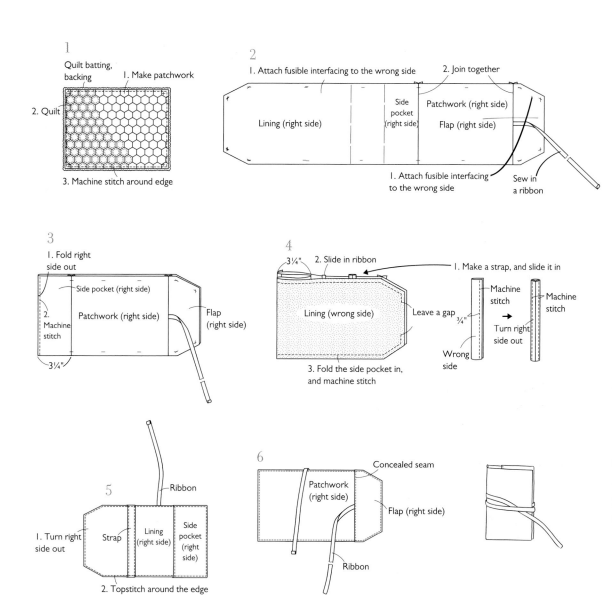

1

Quilt batting, backing

1. Make patchwork

2. Quilt

3. Machine stitch around edge

2

1. Attach fusible interfacing to the wrong side

2. Join together

Lining (right side)

Side pocket (right side)

Patchwork (right side)

Flap (right side)

1. Attach fusible interfacing to the wrong side

Sew in a ribbon

3

1. Fold right side out

Side pocket (right side)

2. Machine stitch

Patchwork (right side)

Flap (right side)

3¼"

4

3¼"

2. Slide in ribbon

1. Make a strap, and slide it in

Lining (wrong side)

Leave a gap

Machine stitch

Machine stitch

¾"

Turn right side out

Wrong side

3. Fold the side pocket in, and machine stitch

5

Ribbon

1. Turn right side out

Strap

Lining (right side)

Side pocket (right side)

2. Topstitch around the edge

6

Concealed seam

Patchwork (right side)

Flap (right side)

Ribbon

Water Bottle Cover

⟨ S E E   P H O T O G R A P H   O N   P A G E   3 9 ⟩

Materials (makes 1)

* Fabric for patchwork (assorted prints): (172) 1⅜" × 1½"
* Fabric for cover top and bottom (piqué): (1) 11¼" × 5¾" and (1) 4½" × 4½"
* Fabric for the lining (insulating fabric such as Insul-Bright): (1) 11¼" × 8"
* Fabric for the backing: (1) 11¼" × 8" and (1) 4½" × 4½"
* Quilt batting: (1) 11¼" × 8" and (1) 4½" × 4½"
* Ribbon: (1) ⅜" × 11¾" long
* Cord: (1) ⅛" × 11¾"
* Buttons: (2) ¾" in diameter

Instructions

1. Using the pattern on page 115 and following the instructions on pages 46–51, sew the patchwork pieces together to form the outer bottle cover (leaving seven hexagons for the bottle cover bottom). Layer the backing, quilt batting, and bag front. Mark the quilting lines, and machine quilt as shown. Machine stitch around the edge of the patchwork, trimming the fabric to size.

2. Layer the backing, quilt batting, and outer fabric for the bottle cover bottom, and machine quilt. Sew together seven hexagonal pieces. Appliqué the patchwork to the bag bottom, and quilt.

3. Fold the patchwork in half, right sides together. Sew the side, and press open the seam. Place the outer bottom fabric on the patchwork, right sides together, and sew around the bottom edge. Repeat this process for the lining.

4. Fold the top fabric in half, right sides together. Sew along the side, leaving a 1" gap in the center of the seam. Press open.

5. Place the lining over the patchwork fabric, wrong sides together. Place the top fabric over the lining, right sides together. Sew around the top edge. Fold up the bottom edge of the top fabric by ⅜".

6. Turn the cover right side out. Fold the top fabric in half toward the outside of the cover, wrong sides together. Sew around the top of the cover ½" from the edge; sew another line ⅛" above this. Sew the bottom edge of the top fabric to the patchwork using a blind stitch (see page 63). Cover this seam with a piece of ribbon, using a blind stitch to sew it in place.

7. Pull the cord through the gap in the top fabric. Knot the ends, and sew two buttons together over the cord.

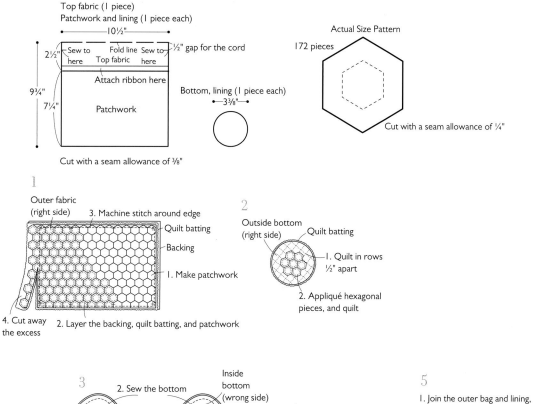

Top fabric (1 piece)
Patchwork and lining (1 piece each)

|← 10½" →|

2½" Sew to here   Fold line   Sew to here   ½" gap for the cord
                  Top fabric

Attach ribbon here

9¾"

7¼"   Patchwork

Bottom, lining (1 piece each)
|← 3⅜" →|

Cut with a seam allowance of ⅜"

Actual Size Pattern

172 pieces

Cut with a seam allowance of ¼"

1

Outer fabric
(right side)   3. Machine stitch around edge
                                Quilt batting
                                Backing
                                1. Make patchwork

4. Cut away   2. Layer the backing, quilt batting, and patchwork
the excess

2

Outside bottom
(right side)   Quilt batting
                    1. Quilt in rows
                    ½" apart

2. Appliqué hexagonal
pieces, and quilt

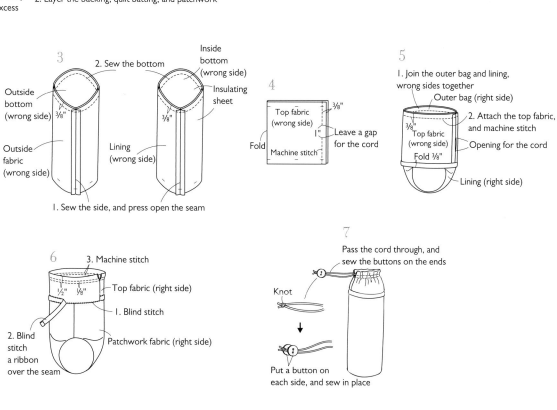

3

Outside bottom
(wrong side) ⅜"   2. Sew the bottom
                                        Inside bottom (wrong side)
                                        Insulating sheet
Outside
fabric
(wrong side)   ⅜"   Lining (wrong side)

1. Sew the side, and press open the seam

4

Top fabric (wrong side)   ⅜"
Fold   1"   Leave a gap for the cord
      Machine stitch

5

1. Join the outer bag and lining, wrong sides together
                    Outer bag (right side)
⅜"   2. Attach the top fabric, and machine stitch
Top fabric (wrong side)   Opening for the cord
Fold ⅜"
                    Lining (right side)

6

3. Machine stitch
½" ⅛"   Top fabric (right side)
        1. Blind stitch
2. Blind stitch a ribbon over the seam   Patchwork fabric (right side)

7

Pass the cord through, and sew the buttons on the ends

Knot

Put a button on each side, and sew in place

115

Octagon Patchwork Shoulder Bag
{SEE PHOTOGRAPH ON PAGE 41}

Materials (makes 1)

* Fabric for the outer bag and handles (striped): (2) 20½" × 18½", (4) 1¾" × 10½"
* Fabric for the patchwork (assorted prints): (100) 1¼" × 1¼", (72) 2¼" × 2¼"
* Fabric for the lining and pocket (print): (2) 20½" × 18½", (1) 15½" × 12¼"
* Fabric for the backing: (2) 20½" × 18½"
* Quilt batting: (2) 20½" × 18½"
* Leather straps for handles: (2) ½" × 8"
* Fusible interfacing: (1) 15½" × 6½"

Instructions

1. Using the pattern on page 119 and following the instructions on pages 48–51, sew the patchwork pieces together as shown to form one patchwork panel each for the bag front and bag back. When connecting the squares and octagons, sew ○ to ○ as shown on the patterns; do not sew across the seam allowance. Fold under the seam allowance around the edge.

2. Layer the backing, quilt batting, and bag front. Mark the quilting lines, and machine quilt as shown. Place one patchwork panel on the bag front, and appliqué in place using a blind stitch. Machine quilt around the seams. Repeat this step for the bag back.

3. Following the instructions on page 107, make the pocket and sew it to the lining.

4. Place the lining pieces right sides together. Sew along the sides and bottom, leaving a gap in the bottom edge. Do not stitch along the cut-out corners. Repeat this step for the outer bag, without sewing a gap in the bottom edge.

5. Press the seams of the lining open, and flatten the bag bottom so that the raw edges along the bottom and the side align. Sew across the edge. Repeat this step for the outer bag.

6. Turn the outer bag right side out. Prepare one long handle by taking two pieces of fabric and folding the long edges in to the center. Place the two pieces wrong sides together, and stitch along both sides of the long edge. Repeat this process for the other handle. Baste the fabric and leather handles to the right side of the outer bag. Place the lining over the bag, right sides together, and sew around the bag opening. Turn the bag right side out through the gap in the lining. Sew the gap closed with a blind stitch (see page 63).

7. Topstitch around the opening of the bag.

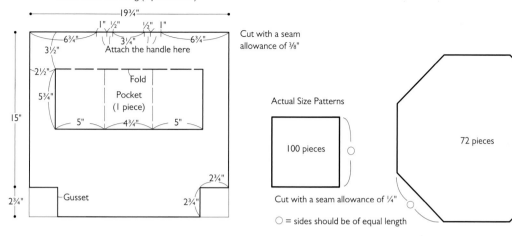

Outer fabric and lining (2 pieces each)

19¾"

1" ½"   ½" 1"

6¾"   3¼"   6¾"

Attach the handle here

3½"

2½"

Fold

Pocket
(1 piece)

5¾"

5"   4¾"   5"

15"

2¾"

Gusset

2¾"

2¾"

2¾"

Cut with a seam
allowance of ⅜"

Actual Size Patterns

100 pieces

Cut with a seam allowance of ¼"

○ = sides should be of equal length

72 pieces

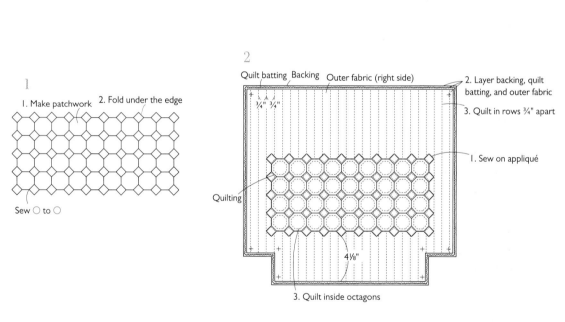

1

1. Make patchwork   2. Fold under the edge

Sew ○ to ○

2

Quilt batting Backing   Outer fabric (right side)

¾" ¾"

Quilting

4⅛"

2. Layer backing, quilt
batting, and outer fabric

3. Quilt in rows ¾" apart

1. Sew on appliqué

3. Quilt inside octagons

119

3

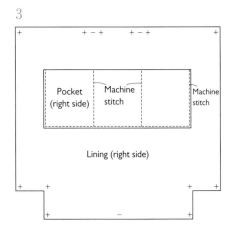

Pocket
(right side)

Machine
stitch

Machine
stitch

Lining (right side)

4

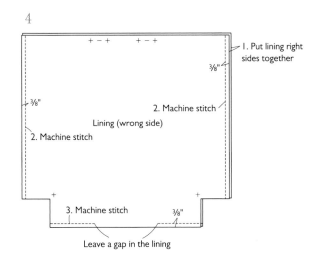

1. Put lining right
sides together

3/8"

3/8"

2. Machine stitch

Lining (wrong side)

2. Machine stitch

3. Machine stitch

3/8"

Leave a gap in the lining

5

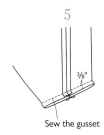

3/8"

Sew the gusset

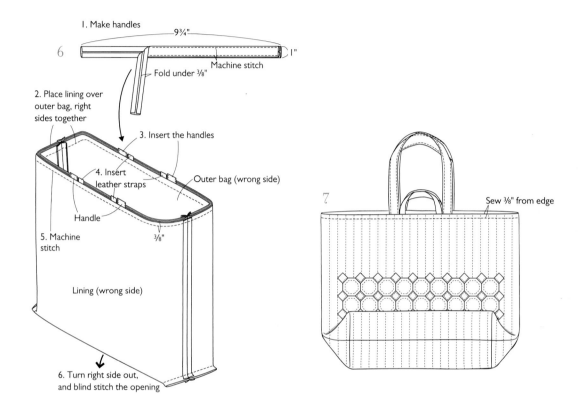

6

1. Make handles

9¾"

1"

Machine stitch

Fold under ⅜"

2. Place lining over outer bag, right sides together

3. Insert the handles

4. Insert leather straps

Outer bag (wrong side)

Handle

⅜"

5. Machine stitch

Lining (wrong side)

6. Turn right side out, and blind stitch the opening

7

Sew ⅜" from edge

Courthouse Steps Zipper Bag

⟩ S E E P H O T O G R A P H O N P A G E 4 2 ⟨

MaterIaLs (maKes 1)

* Fabric for the top panel, opening, and gusset (broadcloth): (2) 14¼" × 2¾"; (2) 2¼" × 21¾"; (2) 4¼" × 11¼"
* Fabric for bottom panel (print): (2) 14¼" × 2¾"
* Fabric for patchwork a (print): Strips of fabric ⅞" wide in varying lengths
* Fabric for patchwork b (print): Strips of fabric ⅞" wide in varying lengths
* Fabric for the handle (plain): (2) 11" × 5"
* Fabric for the backing: (2) 14¼" × 8¼"
* Fabric for the lining and the pocket (print): (2) 14¼" × 8¼", (2) 2¼" × 21¾"; (2) 4¼" × 11¼", (1) 7¾" × 7¾"
* Fusible interfacing: (1) 7¾" × 7¾"
* Fabric for the bias binding: (2) 1" × 42⅜"
* Quilt batting: (2) 14¼" × 8¼"; (2) 11" × 5"; (2) 2¼" × 21¾"; (2) 4¼" × 11¼"
* Zipper: (1) 20"

InstructIons

1. Using the pattern on page 125 and following the sidebar on page 123, make four courthouse steps squares for the bag front. Sew the four patchwork pieces together as shown. Sew the outer fabric to the top and bottom of the patchwork. Layer the backing, quilt batting, and outer bag, and trim the bag front to size. Baste along the seams, and machine quilt. Repeat this step for the bag back.

2. Layer the backing, quilt batting, and outer opening fabric. Machine quilt in rows down the length of the fabric. Place the outer gusset fabric, right sides together, and sew along one short side. Press open. Layer the backing, quilt batting, and outer gusset fabric, and machine quilt as for the opening fabric.

3. Layer the lining (right side up), the zipper, and the opening fabric (wrong side up). Sew along the long edge. Fold the lining and opening fabric open, aligning the fabrics along the cut edges. Sew along the edge of the zipper, and machine quilt the opening fabric. Repeat this process for the other side of the zipper. Layer the gusset lining right side up, the bag opening right side up, and the outer gusset wrong side up. Sew along one short edge. Fold back the outer gusset and gusset lining. Fold under the short edge of the outer gusset and gusset lining by ⅜". Place the ends of the gusset over the end of the opening, and sew them in place to form a loop.

4. Following the instructions on page 107, make the pocket and sew it to the lining.

5. Prepare the two handles by placing the quilt batting on the wrong side of the handle fabric. Fold one edge of the fabric up and over the quilt batting 1¼". Fold the other edge down 1¼" twice. Machine quilt the handle.

Place the front lining and bag front wrong sides together, and baste around the edge on all four sides. Baste the handles in place. Repeat this process for the bag back.

6. Place the bag front and gusset wrong sides together and sew along four sides. Repeat this step for the bag back. Following the instructions on pages 54–55, cover the seam allowances with bias binding. Fold under the seam allowance, and sew to the lining with a blind stitch (see page 63). Turn the bag right side out through the zipper.

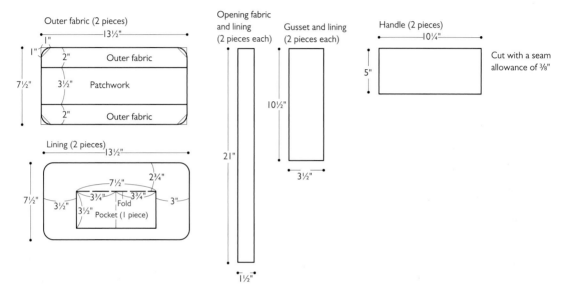

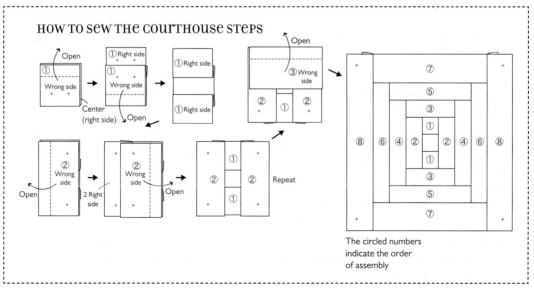

HOW TO SEW THE COURTHOUSE STEPS

The circled numbers indicate the order of assembly

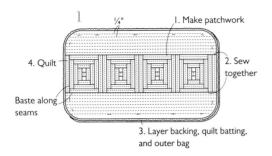

1

1. Make patchwork

¼"

4. Quilt

2. Sew together

Baste along seams

3. Layer backing, quilt batting, and outer bag

2

¼"

Quilt batting

Outside opening fabric (right side)

Backing (wrong side)

1. Sew together

Quilt batting

Backing (wrong side)

2. Quilt in rows ¼" apart

Outside gusset (right side)

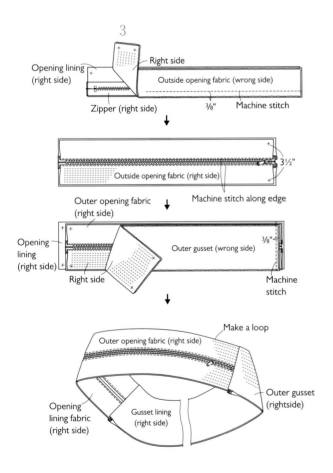

3

Opening lining (right side)

Right side

Outside opening fabric (wrong side)

Zipper (right side)

⅜"

Machine stitch

3½"

Outside opening fabric (right side)

Machine stitch along edge

Outer opening fabric (right side)

Opening lining (right side)

Outer gusset (wrong side)

⅜"

Right side

Machine stitch

Make a loop

Outer opening fabric (right side)

Outer gusset (rightside)

Opening lining fabric (right side)

Gusset lining (right side)

4

Lining (right side)

Pocket (right side)

Sew pocket to lining

5

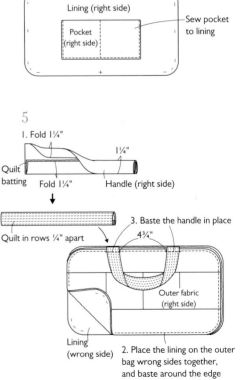

1. Fold 1¼"

1¼"

Quilt batting

Fold 1¼"

Handle (right side)

Quilt in rows ¼" apart

3. Baste the handle in place

4¾"

Outer fabric (right side)

Lining (wrong side)

2. Place the lining on the outer bag wrong sides together, and baste around the edge

6

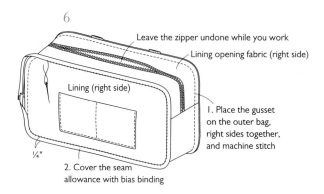

Leave the zipper undone while you work

Lining opening fabric (right side)

Lining (right side)

1. Place the gusset on the outer bag, right sides together, and machine stitch

¼"

2. Cover the seam allowance with bias binding

Actual Size Pattern   Make 8

a

a

a

a

b   b   b   b   b   b   b   b   b

a

a

a

Cut with a seam allowance of ¼"

Resources

Fabric Depot
700 SE 122nd Ave
Portland, OR 97233
(503) 252-6267
www.Fabricdepot.com

Grayline Linen
260 West 39th Street
New York, NY 10018
(212) 391-4130
www.Graylinelinen.com

Purl Soho
459 Broome St.
New York, NY 10013
(212) 420-8798
www.Purlsoho.com

Reprodepot Fabrics
(413) 527-4047
www.Reprodepot.com
Online retailer based
in Easthampton, Mass.

Tall Poppy Craft
(212) 813-3223
www.Tallpoppycraft.com
Online retailer based in New
York City.

U-Handbag
+44 0-208-3103612
www.U-handbag.com
Online retailer based in
London.

About the Author

Suzuko Koseki was born in Tokyo and graduated from Bunka Fashion College. She has been study-ing patchwork since 1978. She studied with Chuck Nohara and taught at the Hearts and Hands Patchwork School. She is currently director of the La Clochette Project. She offers small-group quilting classes at her home, as well as at Asahi Cultural Center in Tachikawa and the Vogue Quilt Institute. Her other books include *Patchwork Style* and *Delightful Patchwork*, both published by Bunka Publishing Bureau; *Japanese Patchwork* and *What I Treasure*, published by Nihon Vogue-sha; and *Patchwork Lessons with Floral Patterns*, published by Japan Broadcasting Publishing Co., Ltd. Her website is http://kwne.jp/~clochette

Trumpeter Books
An imprint of Shambhala Publications, Inc.
Horticultural Hall
300 Massachusetts Avenue
Boston, Massachusetts 02115
www.shambhala.com

Originally published as *Quilt de tuzuru hibi* in 2008 in Japan by Bunka Publishing
Bureau, Tokyo. World English translation rights arranged with Bunka Publishing
Bureau through The English Agency (Japan), Ltd.

Translation © 2011 by Shambhala Publications, Inc.
Translated by Karen Sandness
Bunka Staff Credits: Art Direction: Mihoko Amano; Photography: Miyako Toyoda;
Styling: Nami Kagiyama; Hair and Makeup: Kiko Suzuki (Mods Hair); Model: Rachel;
Tracing: day studio (Satomi Dairaku); Production Assistance: Kayo Urano, Naoko
Taguchi, Keiko Miyamoto, Akiko Nishikawa, Kazuko Tsuji, Eriko Yoshino; Instructions:
Iku Kagawa, Kumiko Kurokawa; Editor: Tomoe Horie.

9 8 7 6 5 4 3 2 1

First English Edition
Printed in China

⊗This edition is printed on acid-free paper that meets the American National Stan-
dards Institute z39.48 Standard.
♻Shambhala Publications makes every effort to print on recycled paper. For more
information please visit www.shambhala.com.
Distributed in the United States by Random House, Inc., and in Canada by Random
House of Canada Ltd
Designed by Daniel Urban-Brown

Library of Congress Cataloging-in-Publication Data

Koseki, Suzuko.
Natural patchwork: 26 stylish projects inspired by flowers, fabric,
and home/Suzuko Koseki.
   p. cm.
ISBN 978-1-59030-881-3 (pbk.: alk. paper)
1. Patchwork—Patterns. 2. Quilting—Patterns. I. Title.
TT835.K6725 2011
746.46—dc22
2010033215